HANDLING A
PERSONAL INJURY
AUTO ACCIDENT CLAIM
FROM CAR WRECK TO SETTLEMENT CHECK

An Attorney Training Manual That Goes Step by Step
Through a Mock Personal Injury Case

CLARENCE B. LEATHERBURY

Printed in the United States of America.

ISBN 979-8-218-83011-3

To my Father

ATTORNEY DOUGLAS CLARENCE LEATHERBURY

Douglas C. Leatherbury, a native of Bennington in Switzerland County, Indiana, has practiced law for more than five decades.

In the 1960s, Doug Leatherbury attended Indiana University, where he earned a bachelor's degree with a major in history and a minor in government. After completing his undergraduate studies, he spent a year teaching fifth grade before enrolling at the Indiana University School of Law.

He received his Doctor of Jurisprudence in 1968 and has since provided legal counsel in more than 7,000 cases. Doug has served as the elected Prosecutor for Switzerland County, Indiana, and currently serves as President of the Washington County Bar Association. He continues to practice law at his general practice firm located at 201 N. Main Street in Salem, Indiana, just steps from the historic Washington County Courthouse.

Doug is the proud father of three children: Suzanne, Whitney, and Clarence. When not practicing law, he enjoys spending time on his 355-acre farm in Tobinsport, Indiana, located along the banks of the Ohio River.

TABLE OF CONTENTS

ABOUT CLARENCE LEATHERBURY & THE BOOK

In this comprehensive guide, I'll walk you through litigating a personal injury auto accident claim from beginning to end.

You'll gain hands-on experience in every stage of the process, from conducting a thorough client intake and accident investigation to obtaining medical records and preparing a compelling demand package. You'll learn how to file a lawsuit, send and respond to discovery requests, and how to negotiate a proper settlement. I'll also equip you with the skills necessary to negotiate reductions in medical liens and manage the settlement process, all while providing a deep dive into the statutes, rules, and key cases that shape personal injury claims.

I have a JD and an LLM with a focus in Corporate Law from Indiana University Robert H. McKinney School of Law. After law school, I worked on a ton of personal injury cases, with a top personal injury law firm where I helped settle well over $1,000,000 in personal injury claims in less than two years and have studied over one hundred books and manuals authored by the very best and brightest legal minds on the subject, and as a result can help you gain mastery-level knowledge of this material. My book covering personal injury auto accident claims is the most thorough on the market today—the educational equivalent of working two years for a top personal injury law firm. If you're a law student or recent law school graduate, after reading this book none of your peers will know more than you.

CLIENT INTAKE & PRE-SUIT INVESTIGATION

INTRODUCTION TO MODULE 1

In this comprehensive training manual based on a real-life auto accident case, I'll guide you through the process of litigating a personal injury claim from beginning to end. You'll gain hands-on experience in every stage of the claims process, from conducting a thorough client intake and accident investigation to obtaining medical records and preparing a compelling demand package. You'll learn about filing a lawsuit, sending and responding to discovery, and negotiating a proper settlement.

This manual will also equip you with the skills necessary to negotiate reductions in medical liens, while providing a deep dive into the statutes, rules, and key cases that shape personal injury claims. Whether you're a law student or a practicing lawyer, this manual will equip you with the skills needed to handle a lawsuit like a seasoned litigator.

Most law graduates leave law school with a grasp of legal theory but have yet to draft complaints, file lawsuits, answer discovery, or conduct depositions. This manual fills those gaps, giving you the tools to meet with clients confidently, explain the litigation process, and carry out the legal work with the expertise of a high-level litigator.

Before diving into the material in this book, one of the most valuable pieces of advice I can offer is to build your own personal law library. Whether you focus on personal injury law, family law, or criminal law, accumulating resources specific to your area of practice is essential to becoming an expert in your field.

I have accumulated over 100 books and manuals in both physical and digital formats, covering personal injury. I've conducted multiple searches on Amazon and eBay, and have sifted through the broader internet looking for books and manuals that would benefit me as a personal injury attorney. And over the years, I've also gathered hundreds of personal injury forms that I've come across in books and online.

I also utilize YouTube to watch top personal injury attorneys explain how they develop their cases. To draft this manual, I went through every personal injury book and manual I've accumulated, reviewed all the forms I've personally collected over the years, and watched numerous instructional videos on personal injury law. I also drew on the individual knowledge I gained while working at a top personal injury law firm to create the most substantive, skills-based personal injury manual on the market today.

Now let's go over the fact pattern in our mock personal injury auto accident claim.

OVERVIEW OF THE MOCK PERSONAL INJURY CASE SAMPSON V JAILBREAK

Lisa Sampson is a 20-year-old college student from New Albany, Indiana. At the time of the accident, she was enrolled at Indiana University Southeast, majoring in mathematics. During this time, she was also employed as a cashier at Home Depot in New Albany.

On June 1, 2024, at approximately 11:10 p.m., in Clark County, Indiana, Plaintiff Lisa Sampson was driving south on Penn Street in Jeffersonville, Indiana, returning home after purchasing snacks at a convenience store. She was operating a 2012 red Ford Mustang.

Defendant Snake Jailbreak was traveling east on 8th Street in a 2004 blue Ford F-150 when he ran a red light and struck Lisa's vehicle in the middle of the intersection. Immediately after the collision, Snake fled the scene on foot. The vehicle he was driving was owned by his passenger, Liv Bouvier, who remained at the scene and informed the investigating officer that the driver who fled had been drinking and was known as Snake.

Immediately before the collision, Snake Jailbreak and Liv Bouvier had been drinking at The Enchanted Forest & Music Hall in New Albany. Following the accident, both Lisa and Liv were transported by ambulance to Clark Memorial Hospital for treatment.

Lisa Sampson maintained an automobile insurance policy with Erie Insurance that included Medical Payments (MedPay) coverage, but the policy did not include Uninsured/Underinsured Motorist (UM/UIM) coverage. Lisa Sampson's health insurance was through Anthem Blue Cross Blue Shield. The vehicle that Defendant Snake Jailbreak was driving was owned by Liv Bouvier, who was also his passenger at the time of the accident. Liv Bouvier's vehicle was insured through Unique Insurance.

THE CLIENT INTAKE FORM

One of the first steps in a personal injury case is having your client fill out an intake form. Throughout my experience as a personal injury lawyer, I consistently relied on this initial document to gather crucial information. For instance, when responding to discovery from opposing counsel, I would refer to the intake form to ensure all of my client's main injuries were included in the discovery responses. Similarly, I would use the intake form to confirm insurance coverage.

Whether obtaining a client's employer information, identifying the client's auto insurance carrier, or simply getting the client's address to mail a letter, the intake form offered readily accessible details. Witness and medical provider information were also readily available on this vital document.

While your client completes the intake form, take the opportunity to gather any photos, videos, or crash reports they may have. Additionally, obtain copies of their driver's license and insurance cards.

Keep in mind that a client's memory of the accident may fade over time, so having them fill out the form promptly is crucial. Having the intake form completed soon after the accident ensures that the information about the client's injuries and the details of the accident are as accurate as possible.

While some lawyers favor lengthy, multi-page forms, I prefer a short, concise one that gathers only the most critical information such as the client's contact information, health and auto insurance, employer information, list of injuries, medical providers your client has visited due to the accident, and description of the accident. The intake form can be enhanced by including a section for the client to list "before-and-after witnesses." This section allows clients to identify individuals who can attest to the client's condition both before and after the injury. For instance, in a case where my client was severely injured by a vehicle in a grocery store parking lot, the "before-and-after witnesses" my client provided proved invaluable. I called the witnesses and recorded our conversations as they described the dramatic physical changes my client experienced due to the accident. I then supplied these recordings to defense counsel and later to the mediator. Having your client list "before-and-after witnesses" on the intake form can also be helpful when answering discovery questions later on and preparing the plaintiff's preliminary witness list for filing with the court.

Under the facts of our mock personal injury case, our client, Lisa Sampson, visited our law office just a few days after the accident and completed our client intake form. On the form, she provided her personal details, including her name, address, phone number, Social Security number, and driver's license number. She noted the date of the accident, the responding police department, and stated that she was transported to the hospital by ambulance. Lisa indicated that her vehicle was towed from the scene. She also supplied her employment information and reported missing several days of work due to her injuries.

The intake form included a list of her injuries and the medical providers she had seen as a result of the accident. She identified the make and model of her vehicle, as well as the name of her auto insurance carrier. While she did not know the name of the at-fault driver's insurer, that information can usually be obtained from the officer's crash report. Lisa also provided her health insurance information, and our office made copies of both her health insurance card and her driver's license for our records. In addition, our office took photographs of her visible injuries to help document the extent of her physical condition.

To view the completed intake form containing Lisa Sampson's initial case details, please refer to Exhibit 1.

HIPAA RELEASE FORMS TO OBTAIN MEDICAL RECORDS

During the intake process, be sure to have your client sign a HIPAA authorization form to ensure you are prepared to obtain her medical records and bills when needed. HIPAA, the Health Insurance Portability and Accountability Act, prohibits medical providers from disclosing a patient's medical information to third parties without proper authorization. Accordingly, all requests for medical records must be accompanied by a valid, signed HIPAA release.

During the client intake, our firm had Lisa Sampson sign a blank HIPAA authorization form. We then made several copies of the signed form so we could later insert the names of specific medical providers when requesting her records.

TURNING DOWN CASES

A vital skill for attorneys is the ability to decline a case. During initial consultations, you may encounter prospective clients whose personality or attitude suggests potential challenges during representation. In his book *How to Successfully Litigate a Personal Injury Case*, attorney Andrew Smiley states: "When I have a client who is retaining me who seems vindictive, focused on payment, or simply out for blood or suffering, I gently tell them that I do not believe we are the firm for them." Similarly, in *Winning Personal Injury Cases*, attorney Evan Aidman emphasizes that a key factor in deciding whether to take a case is assessing if the client's problematic personality could hinder effective collaboration.

Turning down cases also depends on the type of law firm you want to run. For example, there are high-volume firms that sign up multiple cases a day. But I also know there are attorneys in the personal injury field who only want cases with significant injuries. I watched one video of an attorney saying that if you went to urgent care after a wreck and then to a chiropractor a few times, he would refer you to another attorney rather than take the case himself. He views himself as a high-dollar lawyer and only wants high-dollar cases.

VALUATION PITFALLS

In my experience, preexisting conditions, minor damage to the plaintiff's vehicle, intervening injuries, duration and frequency of medical care, conflicting diagnoses, and medical records indicating that the plaintiff has fully healed can significantly impact the settlement offer. Regarding minor impact cases, I've sat in mediations where the adjuster pulls out an image of the plaintiff's vehicle and points out the lack of damage. Insurance companies know such cases are hard to win. For example, the trial lawyer Steven Burris in his book *Automobile Accident Cases in Las Vegas*, stated of minor impact cases, "I consider myself a good lawyer, but my track record on winning minor impact cases is only 50-50; yet that is better than most out there."

Regarding conflicting diagnoses, I once handled a case involving a woman who claimed to have a torn labrum in her shoulder. Her primary care physician stated that the MRI confirmed the tear. However, another group of doctors who examined her concluded that no labral tear was present. The liability adjuster, of course, sided with the doctors who denied the tear.

Regarding medical records indicating the patient is fully healed, I had a case where my client was seriously injured after being struck by a vehicle. Despite his ongoing pain and functional limitations, a follow-up medical record from one of his treating physicians, prepared a few months after the impact, stated that he had fully recovered. It was clear from his continually labored gait that this was not accurate, but the insurance company latched onto that doctor's note and used it to downplay the severity and duration of his injuries.

In regards to intervening injuries, I once handled a case involving a client who was injured in a motor vehicle accident. A few months later, one of her medical records noted that she had fallen at a McDonald's and sustained injuries. However, that physician's note did not mention the prior car accident. As a result, defense counsel sought to use the date of her fall at McDonald's (a few months after the car accident) as the cutoff point for calculating her damages from the initial wreck.

Additionally, I have encountered defense attorneys who argued that some of my past clients did not seek enough medical treatment, while in other cases, they claimed the opposite—that my clients sought excessive treatment.

Another major valuation pitfall is preexisting conditions. If your client has a preexisting condition that was aggravated by the auto accident, expect the defense to argue—often aggressively—that the injury is unrelated to the crash. Insurance adjusters and defense counsel will try to reframe the case as one involving only degenerative changes or prior trauma rather than new harm. They'll rely heavily on past medical records, even those from many years ago, to suggest your client's pain or limitations were already present. Be prepared to combat this narrative with clear imaging comparisons, persuasive treating physician testimony, and—if needed—a qualified medical expert who can explain how the crash aggravated your client's condition.

In our mock Lisa Sampson case, several valuation pitfalls were present. Lisa's injuries were exclusively soft-tissue in nature, her outstanding medical expenses—after insurance payments and provider write-offs–totaled only a few thousand dollars, and she missed only a few days of work. Additionally, the defendant's policy limits were just $25,000, which is the statutory minimum in Indiana. Despite these pitfalls, our firm chose to pursue the case because liability was clear, Lisa's medical records substantiated her injuries, and she underwent months of physical therapy. Moreover, Lisa was a young, sympathetic Plaintiff, and the Defendant's conduct–drinking and driving and then fleeing the scene–was particularly egregious.

THE INDIANA OFFICER'S STANDARD CRASH REPORT

The crash report serves as a cornerstone in most personal injury cases. Throughout my experience, I routinely relied on these reports to gather crucial information. Crash reports play a vital role in drafting complaints, identifying officers and witnesses, pinpointing accident locations, and verifying the defendant's insurance carrier.

Exhibit 2 contains a sample Indiana crash report populated with fictitious information for our mock case, including the names of the plaintiff and defendant, vehicle details, a witness to the accident, the accident narrative, and insurance data. The report outlines the circumstances of the collision and identifies the at-fault driver. This report serves as the foundational document for our mock personal injury case that will be explored in detail throughout this text.

To review the crash report, please refer to Exhibit 2.

BUYCRASH.COM

In Indiana, obtaining a copy of a crash report can be done through the website BuyCrash.com. This website allows users to search for reports by entering the state, police department, involved party's last name, and accident date. Once you locate your desired report, a small fee is required to download it.

ATTORNEY FEE

In your fee contract, I recommend setting your contingency fee at 40% of the settlement proceeds, plus reimbursement for all legal expenses your firm incurs. Many attorneys charge 33% and may increase that percentage if a lawsuit is filed. However, when it comes time to negotiate a resolution—particularly during mediation—it can be helpful to remain flexible with your fees. For example, at mediation, I often reduced the 40% fee so the client could receive a larger portion of the settlement and, in turn, be more likely to accept the offer. By starting at 40%, you give yourself some room to adjust the numbers if needed. Another useful strategy comes from Attorney Andrew Smiley, who notes in his book *How to Successfully Litigate a Personal Injury Case* that he often waives his firm's case expenses to help settle a claim before litigation.

KEY CORRESPONDENCE DURING INTAKE

Immediately after taking an auto accident case, you should notify both the defendant's and the plaintiff's insurance companies that you are representing the plaintiff in the claim. According to the crash report, the registered owner of the vehicle driven by the defendant, Snake Jailbreak, is Liv Bouvier. Liv was a passenger in the vehicle at the time of the collision. The crash report indicates that Liv's auto insurance was with Unique Insurance. In the report, it is further noted that Lisa Sampson, the Plaintiff, had auto insurance coverage through Erie Insurance. Lisa's auto policy included medical payments coverage. Because this coverage was in place, it is important to notify her auto insurer, Erie Insurance, of her medical payments claim.

LETTERS OF REPRESENTATION

Here is the text from the representation letter sent by our firm to Lisa's auto insurer Erie Insurance on June 6, 2024:

> Please be advised that this office has been retained to represent Lisa Sampson for injuries sustained in an accident. We intend to make a medical payments claim under the automobile policy. Enclosed is a copy of the Indiana Officer's Standard Crash Report for your reference.
>
> Please be advised that no information should be released without my client's written consent to any person and/or organization other than this law firm and its representatives.
>
> Also, please send to this office a copy of any and all policies which would include the Declaration Pages. Specifically, we need to know the medical payments limits, as well as a copy of that portion of the automobile policy that governs the medical payments coverage. We also ask that you notify this office in writing confirming receipt of this Notice of Representation and send all future correspondence to this office. Should you have any questions, do not hesitate to contact me.

Further, here is the text from the representation letter sent by our firm to Liv Bouvier auto insurance carrier, Unique Insurance on June 14, 2024. The body of the letter to the defendant's auto insurer reads:

> Please be advised that this office represents Lisa Sampson for injuries sustained as a result of an automobile accident with your insured. The driver of your insured's vehicle ran a red light with multiple witnesses and was later arrested for leaving the scene of an accident. I do not suspect you will dispute responsibility. Enclosed is a copy of the Indiana Officer's Standard Crash Report for your reference.

I will forward to you medical bills and reports for my client as soon as they become available. We will keep you posted on significant treatment developments. Also, please inform me of the policy limit on your insured's vehicle and let me know of any other applicable insurance coverages that might pertain to this claim. I have a concern that this is a policy limits case.

Please notify this office confirming receipt of this Notice of Representation. All future correspondence should be sent to me. Please do not hesitate to contact me should you have any questions.

One helpful tip regarding representation letters to the liability insurer comes from Indiana attorney Scott Starr. In an Indiana CLE presentation titled *Common Mistakes Plaintiff's Lawyers Sometimes Make* (ICLEF: *The Automobile Injury Case*), Starr explains that he likes to emphasize in his letter of representation to the liability insurance adjuster that he is willing and ready to provide any information the adjuster may need to evaluate and settle the case. He wrote, "In this letter of representation, plaintiff's counsel should acknowledge that he is aware that the adjuster needs information to evaluate the claim, and that counsel stands ready and willing to cooperate in providing this information to the company...Plaintiff's counsel should ask the examiner what he can do to make the examiner's job less burdensome."

ACKNOWLEDGMENT LETTERS FROM INSURERS

In our mock Lisa Sampson case, the liability insurer, Unique Insurance, sent us a claim acknowledgment letter immediately after receiving our representation letter. In this claim acknowledgment letter, the liability insurance adjuster wrote:

Please accept this acknowledgment of receipt of your letter of representation dated June 14, 2024, related to the above-mentioned loss. Attached is a copy of our insured's declaration page for the date of loss as noted above which discloses our insured's complete policy limits.

> Kindly be advised that our company continues in its investigation and coverage for this accident. In the meantime, we formally request copies of any and all medical bills, medical records, and medical specials, and any and all police report(s) or other investigated reports, property damage documentation, photos, any and all witness statements along with any and all other information you have relevant to this claim. If you are making a loss time/wages claim, please provide the tax return of the accident date, the year before and the year after.

This correspondence from the liability adjuster provides a clear indication of the documentation the adjuster needs in order to evaluate and resolve the claim. It also serves as a valuable guide for how to maximize a potential settlement offer from Unique Insurance.

After sending a Representation Letter to Lisa's auto insurer Erie Insurance, we quickly received a medical payments coverage acknowledgment letter from Erie in return. The letter confirmed that Lisa is enrolled in medical payments coverage, also known as MedPay. MedPay is optional coverage that a vehicle owner can purchase through their auto insurance policy. It helps cover medical expenses resulting from an accident, up to a specified policy limit, regardless of who was at fault. The text of the medical payments claim acknowledgment letter from Plaintiff's auto insurer, Erie Insurance, reads as follows:

> The purpose of this letter is to acknowledge receipt of your letter of representation dated June 6, 2024.

> I would like to advise you that I will be handling the liability investigation for this accident. I would like to request a recorded statement from our insured in regard to this accident. Please give me a call so we can set up a time that is convenient for everyone to take the statement over the phone.

> I would like to advise you that Susy Samuelson will be handling your client's Medical Payments claim. She can be reached at 812-844-8092.

Once again, please give me a call at your earliest convenience so we can schedule a statement over the phone at the number listed below.

The wreck occurred on June 1, 2024, and within a short timeframe, our law firm had the representation letters sent out. And within a few days of the representation letters being sent, we received acknowledgment letters from both the liability insurer and Lisa's own auto insurer. In personal injury cases, acting swiftly is essential. In our mock case, we promptly established clear communication with insurers, started the process for MedPay to begin paying Lisa's medical bills, and enabled the liability insurer to start investigating the claim.

PRESERVATION OF EVIDENCE LETTER

Preserving evidence is critical in personal injury cases, and video surveillance footage can be especially valuable. When visiting the accident scene, look for nearby businesses or public areas with security cameras that may have captured the incident. If possible surveillance footage exists, promptly send a preservation letter, which is a formal notice from the attorney instructing the entity to preserve any video footage that could show the collision.

For our mock Lisa Sampson case, no video surveillance footage exists.

LETTER OF PROTECTION

A plaintiff's attorney may send a letter of protection (LOP) to a medical provider, agreeing that the provider will be paid for the plaintiff's medical treatment out of any future settlement.

When a personal injury victim has good health insurance, it may cover most medical expenses resulting from the accident. However, not all plaintiffs have access to comprehensive health coverage. In these situations, a letter of protection can be crucial—it allows the plaintiff to receive necessary medical treatment while deferring payment until the case is resolved.

Without a Letter of Protection, some providers may refuse to treat the patient or may send unpaid bills to collections. A letter of protection assures the medical provider that they will be paid from the settlement proceeds, allowing the plaintiff to receive care without delay. In my experience, letters of protection are commonly used with chiropractors and physical therapists who frequently treat accident victims and are familiar with the personal injury claims process.

In our mock personal injury case, a letter of protection was provided, at their request, to one of Lisa's treating medical providers, Chambers Medical Group. Chambers Medical Group is a rehabilitation clinic that provides treatments and therapies specifically for car accident victims.

💡 PRACTICE TIP: Insurance Disclosures

Throughout this manual, I'll be offering practice tips that every personal injury litigation attorney should know. One important practice tip involves insurance disclosures. Before a lawsuit is filed, the defendant's auto insurance company is not legally required to disclose its policy limits to the plaintiff's attorney. In other words, unless litigation has been initiated, the insurer can lawfully withhold that information.

That said, many insurers will voluntarily disclose policy limits if asked. I routinely include this request in my letter of representation. Additionally, when speaking directly with an adjuster, they will often provide the limits upon request. In my experience handling cases in Indiana, the most common auto policy limits are $25,000 or $100,000.

LOCATING DEFENDANT'S LIABILITY INSURANCE

When representing a plaintiff in an auto accident case, one of your first tasks will be to identify the defendant's auto insurer. Below are six effective ways to locate the defendant's liability coverage. One method is to purchase a crash report from BuyCrash.com, as these reports typically contain the defendant's insurance information. Another option is to hire a professional search company, which can locate insurance information for a fee. In trucking accident cases, you can use the U.S. Department of Transportation's Federal Motor Carrier Safety Administration public search website to find licensing and insurance details. Additionally, you may submit Indiana Form 53789 to the Indiana Bureau of Motor Vehicles to obtain the negligent driver's insurance information. You can also send a letter to the vehicle owner requesting that they provide their insurance details. And, if the defendant driver is uninsured or underinsured, check to see if your client has UM/UIM motorist coverage, which you can go after.

If you are unable to obtain the at-fault party's auto insurance information—and it is not a hit-and-run situation where the party's identity is unknown, requiring your client to proceed under their own uninsured motorist coverage to obtain compensation—then filing a lawsuit against the at-fault party will be necessary. Once the lawsuit is filed, the at-fault driver's insurance coverage information can be obtained during discovery through standard tools such as interrogatories or requests for production of documents.

In Indiana, insurance companies are not required to disclose policy limits before a lawsuit is filed. However, once litigation begins, Indiana Trial Rule 26(B)(2) permits discovery of those limits. The rule provides:

> A party may obtain discovery of the existence and contents of any insurance agreement under which any person carrying on an insurance business may be liable to satisfy part or all of a judgment which may be entered in the action or to indemnify or reimburse for payments made to satisfy the judgment. Information concerning the insurance agreement is not by reason of disclosure admissible in evidence at trial. For purposes of this paragraph, an application for insurance shall not be treated as part of an insurance agreement.

For our mock Lisa Sampson case, the crash report provided the name of the defendant's auto insurer, Unique Insurance, and the insurance adjuster disclosed the policy limits upon request.

PROPERTY DAMAGE CLAIMS

Now that we have thoroughly covered the intake process, it's important to address the minimum property damage requirements in Indiana. Under Indiana Code § 9-25-4-5, state law requires drivers to carry at least $25,000 in property damage liability coverage. Before July 1, 2018, the minimum requirement was $10,000. While many personal injury attorneys focus primarily on bodily injury claims, some will also assist clients with related property damage claims—often as a courtesy. In our mock personal injury case, Lisa Sampson chose to handle her property damage claim on her own.

PRE-SUIT INVESTIGATION

Now, let's discuss the next phase of handling a personal injury auto accident claim which is the pre-suit investigation process. The pre-suit investigation might seem interchangeable with intake, but there are distinctions. Intake focuses on gathering initial information, signing the fee agreement, and obtaining the crash report, etc. The pre-suit investigation, however, is broader, encompassing all the steps an attorney takes to develop the case before filing suit. This might involve tasks such as interviewing witnesses, obtaining medical bills and records, visiting the accident scene, or hiring an accident reconstruction expert.

FILMING THE ACCIDENT SCENE

At the law firm Morgan & Morgan, their attorneys typically manage around 125 cases at any given time. In a high-volume practice like that, it's simply not feasible to visit the scene of every accident. However, for larger cases—or if you have a more manageable caseload—it's worth making the effort to visit the accident scene and record footage.

Personally, I use a DJI Pocket 2 camera and a DJI Mini 3 drone. In the past, I've used a GoPro and an X-Star Premium drone. All are high-quality cameras capable of filming in high definition. After capturing footage of the accident location, I share screenshots or full video clips with the adjuster or defense counsel. I may also use aerial photos to create accident scene diagrams, which I will include in the demand packet sent to the adjuster.

Most attorneys send only a standard demand letter with medical records attached. But going the extra mile by including aerial photos or video footage of the accident scene can send a strong message—that you're paying close attention to the case and devoting considerable effort to your client's claim.

For Lisa Sampson's case, I visited the scene of the accident, took photographs of the location, filmed the paths of each vehicle, and captured aerial drone footage of the intersection.

GATHERING EVIDENCE: PROMPT ACTION IS KEY

One of my favorite personal injury books is *The Complete Personal Injury Practice Manual* by Al Cone and Verne Lawyer. In it, the authors stress the importance of initiating evidence-gathering efforts immediately after the attorney-client contract is signed. They write:

> "After the employment contract has been executed, it is imperative that the attorney continue the investigation expeditiously. Most attorneys make it a point to go view the scene of the accident. Statements from witnesses should be obtained as early as possible. And if a criminal prosecution has been processed against any of the parties, transcripts of the testimony of such action should be ordered and obtained."

This emphasis on prompt and thorough investigation is echoed by Evan Aidman in his book *Winning Personal Injury Cases*. Aidman highlights the strategic value of eyewitness accounts, writing:

> "A solid eyewitness statement is an effective way to influence an insurance company to honor the claim. Insurance companies are particularly persuaded by statements made by independent witnesses (someone your client never met before the accident)."

Evan Aidman went on to explain in his book that when a witness is favorable, he prepares a written statement for the witness to sign, accurately reflecting their account of the accident.

RESEARCHING THE DEFENDANT: UTILIZING ONLINE RESOURCES

In today's world, every attorney should be conducting online research. In our mock Lisa Sampson case, researching the defendant, Snake Jailbreak, on the website MyCase.in.gov produced significant information. I discovered a lengthy criminal history and confirmed that the defendant faced separate criminal charges for leaving the scene of the accident and driving while intoxicated when he struck Lisa – details that were missing from the crash report obtained through BuyCrash.com. This means there is both a personal injury auto accident claim, and a separate criminal case arising from the June 1st incident. Additionally, the probable cause affidavit from Snake's criminal case, which I downloaded from MyCase.in.gov, provided a much more detailed account of the accident than the crash report.

While standard demand packets typically include a demand letter, crash report, and medical records, for our mock case, I included the defendant's criminal probable cause affidavit and criminal rap sheet in the demand packet. My goal in including this additional documentation was to strengthen Lisa's claim by highlighting the gross misconduct of Snake, and thereby increase the likelihood that the liability adjuster would decide he had better go ahead and offer the full $25,000 policy limit.

The demand letter I submitted to the liability adjuster specifically highlighted my client's young age. This tactic aimed to emphasize the severity of the incident and the egregious nature of the defendant's actions. A young female college student struck by an intoxicated driver–who had been out partying and fled the scene immediately after the wreck–presents a deeply troubling set of facts. A generic demand letter without these details would fail to convey the full seriousness of the claim.

In a personal injury case I handled, a senior-aged client's vehicle was struck by a middle-aged female truck driver. By reviewing the defendant's public social media, I discovered selfies she took while driving an 18-wheeler, along with posts containing offensive language and inappropriate content. I promptly captured screenshots of these posts and sent them to the defense attorney. Within days, the driver's social media account was either deleted or made private. The driving selfie, in particular, likely played a key role in the case's settlement. Had the case proceeded, I could have used the selfie during the driver's deposition to confirm her awareness of rules prohibiting handheld device use while driving, then presented the image to demonstrate her noncompliance. Such online investigations, requiring minimal effort, can significantly influence an insurance adjuster's or defense counsel's desire to pursue settlement.

GATHERING EVIDENCE: ESSENTIAL TASKS

In nearly every case, there are certain evidence-gathering tasks that plaintiff's counsel should complete as early as possible. These tasks not only help establish liability and damages, but they also give the insurance adjuster a clearer picture of the claim and may even shape the tone of the case moving forward. In the pages that follow, I've laid out specific tools and philosophies that go beyond the basics.

ACCIDENT SCENE VIDEO

As plaintiff's counsel, it can be helpful to record yourself driving or walking the routes of the plaintiff's and defendant's vehicles, giving the insurance adjuster a clear view of their paths leading up to the crash. Videos like this can make a client's auto accident claim far more memorable to the adjuster—especially compared to the hundreds of claims where the only visual is a black-and-white diagram in a crash report.

To review the video stills depicting the paths of Lisa Sampson's and Snake Jailbreak's vehicles prior to the collision, please refer to Exhibit 3 for Lisa's vehicle and Exhibit 4 for Snake's.

CLIENT DOCUMENTATION TIPS

Here are two insights from my personal injury book collection that provide strategies attorneys can use to possibly strengthen their clients' claims. The first emphasizes the importance of documenting out-of-pocket expenses, which can help demonstrate the financial toll of the injury. In *The Indiana Crash Book*, author Randall Sevenish stated, "Keep track of [the client's] out-of-pocket expenses related to the accident—pharmacy prescriptions, co-pays, lawn mowing service, etc."

The second recommendation comes from Al J. Cone and Verne Lawyer's book, *The Complete Personal Injury Practice Manual*, which advises lawyers to have their clients keep every medication bottle they have used as a result of their injuries. The rationale is that a box full of empty prescription containers can serve as compelling visual evidence at trial, reinforcing the extent of the client's pain. As the authors explain, "It is imperative that the reason for saving the bottles and containers is that at trial time some containers are dramatic evidence of the consumption of considerable quantities of drugs prescribed by the treating physician."

However, not all attorneys agree with these strategies. In his book *Automobile Accident Cases in Las Vegas*, trial lawyer Steven Burris cautions against focusing on minor financial losses, such as gas receipts or the cost of over-the-counter painkillers, stating that such details amount to "peanuts" and that focusing on them plays into the adjuster's hands. Burris also warns against emphasizing pain medications at trial (unless it is a catastrophic or extremely serious injury), noting that jurors may misinterpret the use of such drugs as a sign of pain medication addiction rather than legitimate need.

INTERVIEWING OFFICERS

In a CLE titled Common Mistakes Plaintiffs' Lawyers Sometimes Make, Indiana attorney Scott Starr advised that plaintiff's counsel should contact the police officers immediately after an auto accident and interview them. A brief conversation with a responding officer can help solidify the details of the wreck and generate ideas for deposition questions later on. Starr also recommended canvassing local media for any coverage or information about the accident.

BEFORE-AND-AFTER WITNESSES

One often-overlooked but highly effective category of evidence is testimony from "before-and-after" witnesses. These individuals—typically the plaintiff's close friends, family members, coworkers, or neighbors—can provide powerful statements or trial testimony comparing the plaintiff's life before and after the accident. They can describe in vivid, personal detail how the plaintiff's personality, physical abilities, social life, or emotional well being changed following the injury. It's best to interview these individuals early in the case and obtain recorded statements to share with the adjuster or defense counsel. Their testimony can humanize your client and highlight the real-world impact of the injuries in a way that medical records and billing statements cannot.

MYCASE.IN.GOV

I rely on the website MyCase.in.gov more than any other site in the practice of law. Through MyCase.in.gov, attorneys can access case dockets to review filings submitted by opposing counsel and view scheduled court dates. The site also allows users to search other cases that may be relevant to their own. For example, you can determine whether the defendant in your motor vehicle accident case is facing criminal charges arising from the accident. Additionally, I have used this resource to research prominent personal injury attorneys in Indiana and examine the types of pleadings they file in their cases.

ONLINE RESEARCH

While social media can be a valuable source of information, other publicly available online resources can be equally useful. Conducting a compre-hensive internet search—particularly using platforms like Google—can help uncover relevant background information about the opposing party.

For example, in our mock case, googling Snake Jailbreak and potentially locating a mugshot of him being booked for hitting Lisa and then fleeing the scene, certainly would have caught the liability adjuster's attention. However, in our mock claim, no such mugshot exists – which is good news for Snake.

ACCESS TO PUBLIC RECORDS ACT

The police or sheriff's department typically maintains more documenta-tion about a motor vehicle accident than just the standard crash report. Indiana's Access to Public Records Act (APRA), codified as Indiana Code § 5-14-3, grants the public the right to inspect and copy public records, including many documents maintained by law enforcement. The statute affirms that individuals have the right to access information concerning the affairs of government and the official acts of public officials and employees. It also imposes a duty on public agencies to provide access to such records, subject to certain exceptions.

An attorney can use Indiana's Access to Public Records Act to request various types of documentation related to an accident. These may include 911 audio recordings, video footage, computer-aided dispatch (CAD) reports, dashcam and body cam recordings, police photographs, toxicology reports, and other relevant materials.

OBTAINING AND USING TAX RETURNS

During the discovery phase of a personal injury case, defense counsel may request copies of your client's tax returns. Fortunately, clients can obtain their tax transcripts at no cost through the IRS website at https://www.irs.gov/individuals/get-transcript. The site allows individuals to download and view transcripts instantly after verifying their identity. The two most relevant transcript types for discovery purposes are the Return Transcript, which shows key line items from the originally filed 1040 (including total income, adjusted gross income, and basic wage and business income figures), and the Wage and Income Transcript, which reports income sources such as W-2s and 1099s as submitted to the IRS by employers and payers. If full copies of filed tax returns (including all attached schedules and forms) are needed, clients can request them from the IRS using Form 4506. This form provides an exact photocopy of the return as it was originally filed.

Having your client's tax returns on hand can also serve as valuable evidence to support their lost wage claim because tax returns provide an official record of the client's income before the accident. Tax documents, such as W-2s or 1099s, show the client's earnings from employment or self-employment, establishing a clear baseline for their pre-accident income. This helps quantify the financial impact of wages lost due to injuries. Because tax returns are filed with the government under penalty of perjury, they are highly credible in court and reduce disputes over the client's claimed income. Additionally, tax returns provide a multi-year view of income, which is useful for demonstrating consistent earnings or an upward trend over time. This can further strengthen claims for future lost wages or diminished earning capacity. However, additional wage documentation will usually be necessary to fully substantiate your client's lost wage claim to the liability insurer, and we will address those materials in a later section of the book.

For our mock Lisa Sampson case, Lisa's returns were produced in our responses to the Requests for Production of Documents served by defense counsel.

"DAY IN THE LIFE" VIDEOS: DEMONSTRATING IMPACT OF INJURIES

By hiring a professional company to produce a "Day in the Life" video in cases involving serious injuries, you can significantly enhance an adjuster's or jury's understanding of your client's condition and daily challenges. Below, I've included a list of scenes you'll want to feature in the video. These include clear footage of your client's visible injuries, as well as documentation of routine daily activities such as getting dressed, preparing food, and performing personal hygiene tasks. It's also important to show any medical devices your client uses, such as crutches or casts, and to include scenes of wound care or other medically related routines. Additionally, consider including heartfelt testimony from your client about the challenges they face in caring for their children or maintaining relationships with family and friends. As a best practice, the video should be kept to 15 minutes or less.

Beyond their use in the courtroom, it's important to recognize that these videos can also be powerful tools during settlement negotiations and mediation. When provided to the adjuster in advance of a scheduled mediation—or as part of settlement discussions—a well-crafted day-in-the-life video can vividly illustrate the impact of the injury on your client's daily routine. This can greatly enhance the value the adjuster places on the case, thereby prompting a more favorable outcome.

For our mock Lisa Sampson case, her injuries were not near serious enough to warrant a "Day in the Life" video.

SURVEILLANCE VIDEO

When handling a personal injury claim, be aware that the liability insurer may hire an investigator to monitor your client through video surveillance. I recall a personal injury case from my childhood when my father, Doug Leatherbury, represented a client who was secretly recorded loading wood into a truck. The defense attorneys presented this footage to the jury to cast doubt on the seriousness of his purported injuries. In another situation, a colleague of mine at Isaacs & Isaacs represented a man who was severely injured when a dump truck collided with his Ford Ranger. The liability insurer representing the trucking company in that case hired an investigator who filmed the plaintiff painting the underside of a boat at his business. The defense introduced this footage at trial, and the jury ultimately awarded a figure substantially lower than the pretrial offer — likely due in large part to this surveillance footage.

If your client suspects they are being surveilled, consider employing a tactic shared by renowned Georgia personal injury trial lawyer Mike Rafi. He recommends immediately emailing defense counsel to warn that the investigator's conduct amounts to harassment and stating that you will advise your client to file a police report if the surveillance continues. Regardless of whether the surveillance was improper, you should file a motion in limine to exclude the footage from trial. This strategic step can prevent the jury from viewing potentially prejudicial video and improve your client's chances of a favorable outcome.

RECORDED STATEMENTS: DIFFERING LEGAL OPINIONS

Another issue you will encounter as a personal injury attorney is whether your client should provide a recorded statement to the liability adjuster. Opinions on this topic vary widely. Attorney Thomas Benton, in his *Personal Injury Boot Camp CLE*, advised that the general rule is no when dealing with liability adjusters. This position is echoed by Guy Di Martino in his book *A Guide to Indiana Car Accident Claims*, where he agrees that plaintiffs should typically avoid giving recorded statements to the opposing insurer. Steve Burris, in his book *Automotive Accident Cases in Las Vegas*, vehemently opposes allowing your client to give a recorded statement to liability, writing, "It can only be used against you, it can never be used in your favor." However, in a CLE presented by attorney Scott Starr, Starr took a different stance, stating that a plaintiff's attorney should permit a recorded statement in some cases to encourage early settlement. On the matter, Evan Aidman wrote in his book *Winning Personal Injury Cases*, "Under limited circumstances, I permit a pre-suit statement to the other driver's insurance company. If it's a small case and I think I can get it settled without filing suit by cooperating, I might agree."

As you can see, there are a variety of opinions on whether a plaintiff should provide a recorded statement to the liability adjuster. However, if you are dealing with your client's own auto insurance company—such as in cases involving uninsured or underinsured motorist coverage, or MedPay—a statement may be required. This obligation arises from the contractual language in the policy, which the plaintiff likely agreed to when purchasing the coverage.

KEY EXPERTS

Now, let's discuss some of the different types of expert witnesses you can expect to hire as a personal injury attorney. Attorneys often rely on experts to help explain issues of liability, causation, or damages in personal injury cases. While most experts are retained after the lawsuit has been filed, some are hired very early in the pre-suit investigation phase, which is why this section is included in the pre-suit chapter. For example, accident reconstructionists may be brought in immediately after a serious collision to examine the vehicles, review the scene, and preserve key evidence before it disappears. Economic or vocational experts may also sometimes be retained pre-suit to document lost earnings or future care needs if settlement negotiations are anticipated. More commonly, however, experts are hired after the litigation process begins. At that stage, independent medical examiners or specialists—such as radiologists, life-care planners, or vocational experts—are retained to provide deposition and trial testimony.

ECONOMIC EXPERTS

Economic experts are retained in personal injury cases to assess the financial losses suffered by the plaintiff as a result of the accident. Their primary role is to quantify the economic impact of the injuries, focusing on measurable monetary damages such as lost wages, diminished future earning capacity, and the present value of anticipated long-term medical costs.

To project future losses, economic experts frequently rely on mortality tables, which estimate life expectancy based on factors such as age and sex. For example, if a plaintiff has sustained a permanent injury that will prevent them from working for the remainder of their life, the expert will determine the plaintiff's pre-accident remaining work-life expectancy and then calculate the present value of those lost earnings. These calculations often include not only wages, but also fringe benefits, retirement contributions, and other forms of compensation.

While economic experts do not provide medical opinions, they often incorporate data from life care planners or treating physicians to estimate the cost of future medical care. This approach ensures that the projected economic damages reflect the medical realities of the plaintiff's condition.

In cases involving business owners or self-employed plaintiffs, a forensic accountant may be engaged as a specialized type of economic expert. Forensic accountants analyze complex financial records, reconstruct earnings not fully captured by tax returns or pay stubs, and provide a credible, documented account of the plaintiff's pre- and post-accident financial circumstances. Their work is often critical in presenting a complete and accurate damages picture to the jury.

LIFE CARE PLANNER EXPERTS

A life care planner focuses on identifying and documenting the plaintiff's ongoing and future medical and support needs arising from the injury. They are most often retained in cases involving catastrophic or long-term injuries that require continuous care. Drawing on medical records, physician recommendations, and their own clinical expertise, life care planners prepare a comprehensive life care plan detailing the services, treatments, and accommodations the plaintiff will need for the remainder of their life.

A life care plan may include provisions for long-term nursing care, rehabilitation therapies, personal attendant services, home health aides, assistive devices, home or vehicle modifications, psychological services, and medications. The planner evaluates the plaintiff's functional limitations, ability to perform activities of daily living, and capacity to return to work or live independently.

The findings of a life care planner are frequently used by economic experts, who rely on the plan's cost projections and frequency-of-care estimates to assign a dollar value to future medical expenses. In some cases, the life care planner may also opine on life expectancy, especially when injuries are expected to shorten lifespan or increase the need for specialized care. Unlike economists—who typically use mortality tables—life care planners base such opinions on medical evidence and expert consultation.

A life care planner provides a medically supported, comprehensive assessment of the plaintiff's future care needs, along with detailed cost projections for each service, treatment, and support item in the care plan the planner develops. These estimates are based on current market rates and reflect the specific goods and services the plaintiff will need. The life care planner's role is to identify the necessary care and determine its present-day cost. In court, their testimony helps the jury visualize the plaintiff's long-term needs and grasp the full scope and nature of the care required for the rest of the plaintiff's life.

VOCATIONAL REHABILITATION EXPERT

A vocational rehabilitation expert evaluates how a plaintiff's injury affects their ability to work, bridging the gap between medical evidence and real-world employability. They assess the plaintiff's educational background, job skills, employment history, and the physical or cognitive limitations resulting from the injury. This analysis determines what types of work—if any—are realistically available in the labor market given the plaintiff's restrictions.

Using this information, the expert compares the plaintiff's pre-injury earning capacity with their post-injury vocational prospects. The result is an evidence-based assessment of diminished earning capacity, which may include identifying the loss of access to certain occupations, reduced work hours, or the need for lower-paying, less demanding jobs.

Vocational rehabilitation experts often work in conjunction with economic experts, providing the vocational foundation for calculating lost future income. Their testimony can be particularly persuasive in showing the jury the real-world financial consequences of the injury and the long-term effect on the plaintiff's ability to maintain meaningful employment and financial independence.

ACCIDENT RECONSTRUCTIONIST EXPERT

For high-stakes accidents with substantial financial implications, it is often advisable to retain an accident reconstruction expert immediately to investigate the accident scene. These professionals apply principles of physics and engineering to analyze the conditions and events leading to a collision. Their work typically involves examining physical evidence such as skid marks, vehicle damage patterns, roadway design, traffic control devices, and environmental conditions like weather or lighting. In addition, many reconstructionists download and interpret the vehicle's Electronic Control Module ("black box") data, which can reveal speed, braking, steering inputs, and other driver actions in the moments leading up to the crash.

Accident reconstruction experts then synthesize the data collected to determine the sequence of events, identify contributing factors—such as excessive speed, driver reaction times, mechanical failure, or roadway hazards—and assess how the crash occurred. They often prepare scaled diagrams, 3D models, and computer-animated simulations to clearly illustrate their findings. These visual aids can be especially persuasive in helping jurors understand complex crash dynamics.

To gain a deeper understanding of reconstruction methodologies and computer-generated evidence, consult Chapters 29 and 32 of *Truck Accident Litigation*, Second Edition, edited by Laura Ruhl Genson and Anita M. Kerezman, and *Understanding Motor Carrier Claims*, Seventh Edition, by Joseph Fried and Michael Goldberg.

MEDICAL EXPERT

Perhaps the most critical experts in a personal injury motor vehicle accident case are the medical experts. These professionals draw upon their education, training, and clinical experience to diagnose injuries, recommend treatment, and establish causation by offering opinions on whether the plaintiff's injuries were caused by the collision. Their testimony forms the foundation for proving that the accident resulted in specific injuries, that those injuries required and will continue to require medical care, and that compensation for both past and future medical expenses is justified.

Medical experts fulfill several critical functions in personal injury cases. They diagnose injuries with precision, producing detailed medical records that serve as key evidence in court. They also outline necessary treatments—from surgeries to rehabilitation—which help quantify the cost of care. Additionally, they assess the long-term prognosis, determining whether injuries may result in permanent impairment or affect the plaintiff's quality of life. Their testimony is vital, as they explain complex medical concepts in an accessible manner during depositions or trials. By performing these roles, medical experts strengthen the plaintiff's claim and ensure the compensation sought reflects the true extent of the harm suffered.

The choice of medical expert depends on the nature and severity of the plaintiff's injuries. Orthopedic surgeons are often retained to address musculoskeletal injuries such as fractures, torn ligaments, or herniated discs. Neurologists specialize in evaluating brain injuries, including concussions or traumatic brain injuries, as well as spinal cord or nerve damage. Plastic surgeons focus on reconstructive procedures for trauma-related disfigurement, such as scarring or facial injuries. In cases involving chronic pain or long-term impairment, pain management specialists assess ongoing symptoms and recommend therapies to improve quality of life.

Primary care physicians can also play a pivotal role in personal injury motor vehicle accident cases by providing a comprehensive overview of the plaintiff's medical history, pre-accident health, treatment timeline, and continuity of care. Because they often serve as the plaintiff's long-term treating doctor, they are uniquely positioned to connect the accident to the full scope of injuries and to explain how those injuries have affected the plaintiff's overall health. Their familiarity with the plaintiff's baseline condition allows them to identify new or aggravated conditions resulting from the collision. In litigation, primary care physicians are frequently called to testify in cases involving straightforward injuries or where establishing causation and continuity of care is central to the claim. They can walk the jury through the sequence of treatments, referrals to specialists, and ongoing medical needs in plain, relatable terms. Their testimony carries credibility because it comes from a treating physician rather than a retained litigation expert, often making their opinions more persuasive to jurors. By providing an accessible and authoritative narrative, primary care physicians bridge the gap between the plaintiff's medical history and the jury's understanding of how the accident has altered the plaintiff's life.

IMAGING EXPERT

Radiology experts play a pivotal role in personal injury litigation by interpreting diagnostic imaging such as MRIs, CT scans, and X-rays to identify and explain injuries sustained in auto accidents. Their interpretations can provide objective medical evidence linking a traumatic event to physical harm—particularly in cases involving spinal injuries, herniated discs, or soft tissue damage that may not be visible through physical examination alone. When imaging is central to the case, a radiology expert can be essential in diagnosing the injuries and clearly explaining their nature and extent.

These specialists are retained by both plaintiff and defense counsel. Plaintiff's counsel may engage a radiology expert to ensure an independent and thorough analysis of the scans and films. Defense counsel often uses them to challenge the severity of the claimed injuries or to dispute causation—frequently arguing that certain findings, such as degenerative changes, predate the collision.

Radiology experts typically prepare detailed written reports interpreting the imaging results. These reports often address causation by explaining whether the abnormalities seen are consistent with acute trauma from the incident or with pre-existing conditions. Their opinions can carry significant weight in settlement negotiations, mediation, and trial. Clear, well-supported imaging interpretations can help adjusters, mediators, or jurors understand the medical basis for the claimed injuries and how those findings fit into the broader damages picture.

MENTAL HEALTH EXPERT

In cases where a plaintiff suffers emotional or psychological trauma as a result of an accident, a mental health expert can be a valuable component of the case. Psychologists and psychiatrists are trained to evaluate and diagnose conditions such as post-traumatic stress disorder (PTSD), depression, anxiety disorders, or chronic pain syndrome that may develop following a motor vehicle collision.

Their testimony can help a jury understand the full scope of the plaintiff's injuries, especially when those injuries are invisible on medical imaging or physical examination. By explaining how psychological injuries affect daily functioning, relationships, and the ability to work, a mental health expert can provide powerful support for claims involving non-economic damages, such as pain and suffering, loss of enjoyment of life, and emotional distress.

These experts often rely on standardized psychological assessments, structured clinical interviews, and review of medical and mental health records to form their opinions. They may also recommend ongoing therapy, medication management, or other interventions, which can demonstrate the long-term impact of the trauma and the plaintiff's need for continued care. In the courtroom, mental health experts translate clinical findings into understandable terms, giving jurors a clear picture of how the accident has affected the plaintiff's mental and emotional well-being.

MEDICAL PAYMENTS COVERAGE (MEDPAY)

Now let's discuss medical payments coverage, often referred to as MedPay.

MEDICAL PAYMENTS COVERAGE

Medical payments coverage, also known as MedPay, is an optional add-on to commercial auto insurance that provides no-fault benefits, helping the insured and their passengers pay medical expenses after an accident, up to the policy's specified limit. It exists for the direct benefit of the policyholder, ensuring that necessary treatment can be accessed and paid for promptly, regardless of who caused the crash.

MedPay typically pays before a plaintiff's health insurance because it is contractually structured to act as the primary payer for accident-related medical expenses. Most health insurance plans include coordination of benefits clauses that make them secondary to auto-related coverages like MedPay, meaning they will not pay until those primary coverages are exhausted.

Liberty Mutual, on its webpage titled *Medical Payments Coverage*, explains: "If you're in an accident and have medical payments coverage and health insurance, your medical payments coverage will pay for covered expenses related to the accident first. Once you reach the limit of your medical payments coverage, then your health insurance covers the remaining costs." This same point is echoed by Indiana personal injury firm, Hensley Legal Group, which advised on its website that medical bills should be submitted to MedPay before being submitted to the client's health insurance company.

Soon after taking the case, you should determine whether your client has MedPay coverage through their auto insurance policy. If they do not, they may still rely on their private health insurance to receive medical care. It's important to understand that the defendant's liability insurance company will not pay for the plaintiff's medical bills while the case is pending. Instead, your client's medical expenses are typically paid using MedPay, health insurance, or out-of-pocket funds.

As a personal injury attorney representing an injured plaintiff, it is important to send a Notice of Insurance Coverage letter to the client's medical providers early in the case. This letter informs providers of any available medical payments (MedPay) coverage under the client's auto insurance policy, as well as the details of any applicable health insurance. Doing so helps ensure that medical providers bill the correct payer, avoid unnecessary delays, and coordinate benefits properly.

When medical bills are paid through your client's MedPay coverage, the auto insurer that issued the policy generally retains a right of reimbursement—commonly referred to as subrogation—if your client later recovers a settlement from the at-fault driver. However, when you pursue a claim or lawsuit against your client's UM/UIM carrier, that same insurer may agree to waive its MedPay lien as part of the resolution of the UM/UIM claim.

For example, assume your client carries UM/UIM coverage with Progressive Insurance and, following the accident, Progressive paid $5,000 in medical expenses under its MedPay coverage. If you later file a lawsuit against Progressive to recover additional compensation under the UM/

UIM policy and demand $20,000 to settle the claim, Progressive may agree to waive its $5,000 MedPay lien in order to facilitate settlement of the UM/UIM case.

In the course of handling a personal injury case, it's important to understand the sequence of communications and responsibilities that follow the exhaustion of medical payments coverage. Once your client's MedPay coverage has been fully exhausted, the auto insurer will typically send a formal letter to your office confirming that the coverage has been used up. This letter serves as critical documentation for your file. It marks the point at which the plaintiff's auto insurance carrier is no longer responsible for paying any additional medical bills under the MedPay portion of the policy.

After receiving this letter, your responsibility as plaintiff's counsel shifts toward ensuring proper coordination of ongoing medical billing. At this stage, you should send a notice to all of your client's medical providers advising them that the MedPay benefits have been exhausted. This letter should inform providers that no further payments will be made by the plaintiff's auto insurer, and that any future bills should instead be submitted to your client's health insurance carrier.

CASE MANAGEMENT SOFTWARE

Having covered intake and the pre-suit investigation process, it's worth stepping back to consider the system in your office where all of this information will be stored and organized. Every detail—from client forms and medical records to insurer correspondence—should be captured and tracked in one place, which is why case management software is such a critical part of modern personal injury practice.

A solid case management software system—such as Needles or Filevine—centralizes case activity, keeps deadlines and communications organized, and drives efficiency across the firm. The key is to establish clear standards for how the system is used and to ensure that every team member within your firm follows them consistently. All communications related to a case, whether phone calls, emails, or text messages, should be entered immediately into the system. For example, if a client texts that they have begun treating with a new doctor, the staff member receiving the message should update the Medical Provider section right away and create the next tasks to be performed and checked off within the system, such as requesting records, preparing a HIPAA authorization, or notifying the attorney assigned to the case of the new treatment.

All pending tasks, as well as completed ones, should be tracked in the software. This creates a living checklist that reflects the true progress of each case. Programs like Needles allow firms to build customized workflows so that, when a new file is opened, the system automatically generates the standard tasks to be completed, such as sending an opening letter, ordering the police report, and verifying insurance coverage. As tasks are completed, they should be checked off in the system, leaving a clear and reliable record of work performed.

Beyond tracking, case management software also enhances productivity by automating repetitive processes. Standard documents, forms, and letters can be generated with just a few clicks instead of being drafted from scratch.

SUMMARY OF THE LISA SAMPSON CASE FOR MODULE 1

On June 1, 2024, in Jeffersonville, Indiana, Lisa Sampson was injured when defendant Snake Jailbreak ran a red light and struck her vehicle before fleeing the scene. After the collision, Lisa was transported by ambulance to Clark Memorial Hospital. At the time of the accident, Lisa had auto insurance through Erie Insurance with $5,000 in Medical Payments (MedPay) coverage and health insurance through Anthem Blue Cross Blue Shield. The defendant's vehicle was insured by Unique Insurance.

A few days after the accident, Lisa retained our firm and completed a detailed intake form outlining her injuries, medical treatment, employment, and insurance information. She also executed a HIPAA authorization permitting us to obtain her medical bills and records. At the request of Chambers Medical Group, her physical therapy provider, our firm issued a letter of protection guaranteeing payment for Lisa's treatment from any future settlement proceeds.

We promptly sent letters of representation to both the liability carrier, Unique Insurance, and Lisa's auto insurer, Erie Insurance. In response, Unique Insurance issued an acknowledgment letter identifying the documentation required to evaluate the claim, while Erie Insurance provided a Medical Payments Claim Acknowledgment Letter.

Our office notified each of Lisa's medical providers of her available insurance coverage, including MedPay benefits through Erie and health insurance through Anthem. After Lisa had been treating for some time, Erie Insurance confirmed that her $5,000 MedPay limit had been fully exhausted. Upon receiving the exhaustion letter, we promptly sent follow-up correspondence to all of Lisa's medical providers, advising them to submit any future bills to her health insurance carrier, as no additional payments would be made under the MedPay policy.

Our pre-suit investigation included obtaining the crash report and photographs documenting Lisa's bruising. We researched the defendant's background online and confirmed through MyCase.in.gov that criminal charges had been filed against Snake for leaving the scene of the accident. We also took our own photographs and drone footage of the accident scene. In addition, we phoned a witness identified in the crash report and obtained a recorded statement.

END OF MODULE 1

This concludes Module 1. In Module 2, we will discuss medical bills and records.

MEDICAL BILLS & RECORDS

INTRODUCTION TO MODULE 2

Now, let's discuss one of the most important aspects of a personal injury claim: the medical bills and records.

OVERVIEW OF LISA SAMPSON'S MEDICAL BILLS

On June 1, 2024, Lisa Sampson was transported by the Yellow Ambulance Company of Southern Indiana to Clark Memorial Hospital, incurring a charge of $1,000 for the ambulance service.

That same day, she received treatment for her injuries at Clark Memorial Hospital, which billed her $2,500 for its services.

While at Clark Memorial Hospital, Lisa was given X-rays of her hip and wrist by the company Radiology Associates. The total amount charged was $400.

While at the hospital on June 1, 2024, Lisa was prescribed crutches. The crutches came from the medical equipment company Breg, Inc. The total amount charged by Breg, Inc. was $300.

While at the hospital on June 1, 2024, Lisa was prescribed pain medication, which she later picked up at Walgreens. Walgreens charged a total of $100 for the prescription pain medications.

On June 4, 2024, Lisa went to her primary care provider, Strickland, Cox & Associates. The total bill for the visit was $200.

On June 4, 2024, Lisa's primary care provider ordered her to attend physical therapy with Chambers Medical Group. Lisa began her physical therapy on the same date, June 4, 2024, and ended the physical therapy treatment on October 4, 2024. The total cost for Lisa's physical therapy was $8,500.

The total of Lisa's medical bills amounts to $13,000.00. However, as you will see in the coming modules, the actual amount Lisa was responsible for paying out of pocket was substantially less than this total. This decrease was due to payments made by her MedPay coverage and health insurance, as well as medical provider adjustments, contractual write-offs, and negotiated reductions. Figuring these adjustments is crucial when evaluating a client's true financial exposure and the net recovery they can expect from any offered settlement.

MEDICAL AUTHORIZATIONS FROM DEFENSE COUNSEL

Occasionally, defense counsel will request that your client sign authorizations so they can obtain the plaintiff's medical records. These requests are usually appropriate and should generally be honored. However, you will want to ensure that the authorizations are limited to specific medical providers and cover only a defined period of time. The goal of the plaintiff's attorney in this situation is to protect the client's privacy and ensure that only relevant medical information is disclosed.

🔆 PRACTICE TIP: Medical Authorizations

In his book *A Guide to Indiana Car Accident Claims*, Indiana personal injury attorney Guy DiMartino offers practical guidance on handling medical authorizations requested by defense counsel. DiMartino notes that he does not provide blank authorizations to defense counsel. Instead, he limits the scope of authorizations to five years of prior medical records and specifically excludes permission to obtain psychological and communicable disease records. He also avoids signing general blanket authorizations, opting instead to require a separate authorization for each individual provider. This approach allows him to monitor exactly which records the defense is obtaining. Finally, DiMartino requests that defense counsel provide him with a copy of every record they obtain through the authorizations.

🔆 PRACTICE TIP: Documenting Injuries

Here's a good practice tip: advise your client that whenever they visit a doctor for treatment related to a vehicle accident, they should clearly inform the provider that their injuries were caused by the crash. It is essential that this causal connection is documented in the medical records. Insurance adjusters rely heavily on medical documentation to evaluate claims, and if the records do not clearly link the injuries to the accident, it may significantly undermine the case's value.

REQUESTING MEDICAL BILLS AND RECORDS

When handling a personal injury claim, one of the most important tasks is obtaining your client's medical records and medical bills. Although these requests are often sent to the same medical provider, they should be sent as two separate letters. This is considered best practice because hospitals and clinics often have distinct departments that handle medical records and medical billings, and combining the requests can lead to unnecessary delays or confusion.

Each letter should clearly identify the patient, the dates of treatment, and the purpose of the request. The medical records request letter should ask for complete treatment records, including office notes, imaging reports, test results, and any other documentation relevant to the client's care. The medical bills request letter should specifically seek itemized statements or ledgers showing the charges associated with the treatment.

Both letters should include a signed HIPAA-compliant authorization form from your client. This form grants you legal permission to obtain the client's private health information.

Additionally, each request should be accompanied by an affidavit of certification. This document is signed by the custodian of records and affirms that the attached records or bills are true and complete copies maintained in the ordinary course of business. Under Indiana Code § 34-43-1-7, the affidavit must include certain information to be valid, such as the name of the custodian, the description of the documents, and a statement verifying that the records were kept in the regular course of business at or near the time of the event they describe.

Regarding Lisa's medical records, I sent a separate letter to each of her medical providers requesting copies. Other than the medical provider's name, address, and dates of treatment, the text of each letter was identical. The letter stated:

I represent Lisa Sampson in a claim based on personal injuries arising from an accident on June 1, 2024. Please send me a complete copy of any and all medical records from 06/01/2024 through and including the present date. My request and authorization includes:

- ► Medical history forms completed by my client
- ► Emergency room records
- ► Admission and discharge records
- ► Consultation reports
- ► Nurse's notes
- ► X-ray interpretations
- ► Diagnostic imaging films and reports
- ► Surgical and operative notes
- ► Referrals
- ► Impairment ratings
- ► All other documents and statements of any kind or nature

I am enclosing a signed medical authorization form and affidavit of certification for the requested records.

Please send the requested records to the following email address LeatherburyLaw@gmail.com or by fax to 812-883-2210. If you cannot produce the records in an electronic format, please mail the requested documents to me at the address listed in the heading of this letter.

Regarding Lisa's medical bills, I sent a separate letter to each medical provider requesting copies of her itemized statements. Each letter contained the following text:

My law firm represents Lisa Sampson in connection with injuries she suffered in a motor vehicle crash on June 1, 2024. It is our understanding that our client was seen at your facility for these injuries.

Please send an itemized statement for services rendered to Lisa Sampson from 6/01/2024 to the present date. Enclosed is a HIPAA authorization and an affidavit of certification.

At the time of this writing, we believe our client is no longer receiving medical care from you. If I am wrong about this or Lisa Sampson has since gone back for further treatment, please contact us so we may discuss sending all of the records at the conclusion of her treatment.

If possible, please fax the records and/or bills to my attention at (812) 883-2210 or email them to LeatherburyLaw@gmail.com. If you are unable to provide the statements electronically, you may mail them to the address listed in the header of this letter. Should you have any questions or need further assistance, feel free to contact me at (812) 883-2292.

If this request has not been sent to the proper custodian, please let us know where we should send the request. Thank you for your time and assistance.

Of course, the medical records and medical bill request letters discussed above are just a couple examples. The book *Library of New Jersey Personal Injury Forms, Third Edition*, edited by Eric Kahn, contains many excellent samples, as does the *Handbook of Personal Injury Forms and Litigation Materials, Second Edition*, by Edward Swartz and Elly Swartz. In addition, numerous template letters are available online.

☀ PRACTICE TIP: Medical Imaging

Another helpful tip is to make sure you obtain copies of imaging, such as X-rays and MRIs, to include with the demand packet sent to the adjuster. Including imaging can increase the value of a personal injury claim if the images effectively demonstrate the nature and severity of the injuries.

DEFINING MAXIMUM MEDICAL IMPROVEMENT

Understanding the concept of maximum medical improvement is crucial for every personal injury attorney. This term refers to a plateau in a patient's recovery, indicating that they have either fully recovered or that their medical condition has stabilized and is unlikely to improve further with continued treatment.

Once your client reaches maximum medical improvement, you can begin preparing the demand packet to send to the insurance adjuster. It is generally advisable to wait until treatment is complete, as sending the demand while your client is still undergoing care could result in undervaluing the claim and leaving settlement money on the table. However, there are exceptions. One situation where it may be appropriate to send the demand packet before treatment concludes is when your client's damages clearly exceed the available liability policy limits. If such a situation arises, you can state in your demand letter something to the effect, "My client remains treating, his damages, both economic and non-economic, will continue to grow. You now have enough information to tender the limits."

Additionally, if the statute of limitations is approaching and your client is still receiving treatment, you should go ahead and file the lawsuit to preserve the claim. Once your client reaches maximum medical improvement, you can then prepare and send the demand packet.

SUMMARY OF THE LISA SAMPSON CASE FOR MODULE 2

In our mock Lisa Sampson case, the maximum medical improvement date was around October 4, 2024. On that date, Lisa's doctor documented in her medical records that her injuries had healed from the auto accident, and there are no subsequent records that contradict this conclusion. As a result, it is likely that the adjuster would not consider any medical charges incurred after October 4 to be related to the claim. Of course, you should confirm with your client that they have completed treatment before sending out the demand packet.

Our law firm sent separate written requests to Lisa's medical care providers for her medical records and itemized bills, each accompanied by a HIPAA-compliant authorization and an affidavit of certification to be signed by the medical care provider's custodian of records.

END OF MODULE 2

This concludes Module 2. In Module 3, we will cover the topics of liability and insurance.

LIABILITY & INSURANCE

INTRODUCTION TO MODULE 3

For module 3, we are going to have a discussion on liability and insurance.

LIABILITY

To prove fault in Indiana, the victim must show that the at-fault party owed a duty of care to the victim, the duty of care was breached, the injury is a direct result of the breach known as causation, and there were damages.

In his book *Winning Personal Injury Cases*, Attorney Evan Aidman explains that, "You must prove every aspect of negligence law. This includes negligence, causation, and damages. Negligence is the lack of reasonable care that an ordinary person would have taken under similar circumstances. Thus, you must prove that the defendant's behavior was careless or in some way unreasonable. You must also prove that this behavior caused the injury, and you must prove the extent of the damages."

NEGLIGENCE: DUTY, BREACH, CAUSATION, DAMAGES

At the heart of a negligence claim are four essential elements: duty, breach, causation, and damages. First, the plaintiff must establish that the defendant owed them a legal duty of care. This duty arises from the relationship between the parties or the situation at hand—for example, drivers owe a duty to others on the road to drive safely. Second, the plaintiff must show a breach of that duty by demonstrating that the defendant failed to act as a reasonable person would have in the same situation. This is where the reasonable person standard comes into play. It is a legal benchmark used to evaluate whether someone's actions were appropriate under the circumstances. Judges or juries assess the evidence to determine whether the defendant's behavior fell below this standard. If it did, the defendant is considered to have breached their duty of care.

The third element is causation. The plaintiff must prove that the defendant's breach actually caused the injury. This can be both actual cause (also known as "but-for" causation) and proximate cause, which considers whether the harm was a foreseeable result of the defendant's actions.

Lastly, in a negligence claim, the plaintiff must prove damages, meaning they suffered a real loss—such as physical injury, financial costs, or emotional distress—that can be compensated.

ADMITTING FAULT: A DEFENSE STRATEGY

On occasion, before trial, when the defendant's fault for the accident is clear or not worth contesting, the liability insurer may admit that their insured was negligent. In such cases, the trial will primarily focus on determining the amount of monetary damages to be awarded. I had a trial in Floyd County where, just a few days before trial, the defense attorney finally acknowledged that their client was negligent. As a result, the trial focused solely on damages. The defense often admits liability just before trial as a strategic move. By doing so, defense counsel can show remorse for the defendant's negligent acts in front of the jury and appear to take responsibility for what happened. Admitting liability can also shift the focus away from the defendant's conduct, potentially reducing the amount of damages awarded.

PREPONDERANCE OF THE EVIDENCE

In civil cases, the plaintiff has the burden of proof and must prove their claim by a preponderance of the evidence. This means the plaintiff must show that their version of events is more likely true than not—just enough to tip the balance slightly in their favor, beyond the 50% mark. In contrast, the burden of proof in criminal cases is higher because the stakes are often more serious. Since a criminal conviction can lead to imprisonment, the law requires proof beyond a reasonable doubt.

MODIFIED COMPARATIVE FAULT/PURE COMPARATIVE NEGLIGENCE

It's also important to note that Indiana is a modified comparative fault state, as set forth in Indiana Code § 34-51-2-5 and Indiana Code § 34-51-2-6. In a modified comparative fault state, a jury's monetary damage award will be reduced by the percentage of fault attributed to the injured party—but only if their fault does not exceed 50%. If a jury finds that the plaintiff is more than 50% at fault, they are barred from any recovery.

By contrast, Kentucky is a pure comparative negligence state, codified under Kentucky Revised Statutes section 411.182. Under this system, a plaintiff's damages are reduced in proportion to their percentage of fault, regardless of how high that percentage is. For example, in Kentucky, if your client is found 80% at fault and the other driver 20% at fault, your client would still recover 20% of the total damages. So, if the total damages awarded were $100,000, the client would receive $20,000.

CLAIMS AGAINST THE STATE

If your client was injured due to the negligence of the State of Indiana, the claim would be governed by the contributory negligence standard rather than the modified comparative fault standard. This means that if a case involves a government entity or a state employee as the defendant, the stricter contributory negligence rule applies. Under this standard, plaintiffs are barred from recovering damages if they are even 1% at fault for the incident. Therefore, if a plaintiff bears any degree of fault, they are not entitled to recover from the state. The Indiana Tort Claims Act outlines the procedural requirements for suing the State of Indiana.

SPECIAL RULES IMPACTING NEGLIGENCE AND FAULT

When evaluating liability in a personal injury case, it's important to understand how certain legal rules shape how liability is assigned. For example, the eggshell plaintiff principle holds a defendant fully liable for all resulting harm, even if the victim was unusually vulnerable to injury. Further, Indiana's No-Pay, No-Play laws can limit what damages an injured but uninsured driver can claim, which directly affects liability exposure. Finally, the permissive user doctrine clarifies when an owner's insurance covers someone else's negligence behind the wheel. Together, these principles help define the true reach and limits of liability in auto accident cases.

THE EGGSHELL PLAINTIFF

The eggshell plaintiff principle, also known as the eggshell skull rule or thin skull rule, is a fundamental concept in tort law that applies to personal injury cases. This doctrine holds that a defendant is liable for the full extent of a plaintiff's injuries, regardless of any preexisting conditions that may have made the plaintiff more vulnerable to harm. Under this principle, the defendant must take the plaintiff as they find them. Consequently, defendants cannot reduce their liability by arguing that the plaintiff's injuries—though exacerbated by the incident—were unusually severe due to prior health conditions. This rule ensures that the law protects individuals with preexisting vulnerabilities and holds wrongdoers accountable for the actual harm caused, regardless of the plaintiff's prior state of health.

If your client has preexisting injuries, consider explaining the *eggshell plaintiff* principle in your demand letter to the insurance adjuster and citing supporting Indiana case law. Insurers frequently rely on preexisting conditions to deny claims or justify low settlement offers. In many cases I have handled, an adjuster or defense counsel has argued that my client's injuries were primarily caused by prior conditions. In such situations, it can be effective to include direct quotations from Indiana case law emphasizing that a defendant is liable for the degree to which their conduct aggravated a plaintiff's preexisting condition.

Now, let's use a hypothetical scenario to explain the eggshell skull rule. Imagine you're driving down the road at 25 miles per hour and, unfortunately, you rear-end another car. Inside that car is Sarah, a paraplegic with limited mobility due to a prior spinal cord injury. While a 25-mile-per-hour impact might not seriously injure the average person, it could significantly worsen Sarah's preexisting condition. Under the eggshell skull rule, even though Sarah's prior injury made her more susceptible to harm, you—as the defendant—would still be liable for the full extent of her aggravation, because you caused the accident.

Now, for a slightly humorous twist: imagine that instead of Sarah, you rear-end a different car under the exact same conditions. This time, the driver is none other than the 7-foot-tall, 350-pound Shaquille O'Neal. In this version of events, Shaq might walk away completely unharmed. But Sarah, under the same circumstances, could suffer severe injuries due to her preexisting paraplegia.

The key takeaway is that the eggshell skull rule protects people with preexisting conditions. They shouldn't be penalized simply because their bodies react differently to trauma. The defendant is responsible for the harm they caused, regardless of the victim's unique vulnerabilities.

NO PAY, NO PLAY LAWS

You should also be aware of Indiana's No-Pay, No-Play laws, found in Indiana Code § 34-30-29.2 and Indiana Code § 27-7-5.1. These laws were enacted to encourage motorists to purchase and maintain auto insurance.

Under Indiana's No Pay, No Play laws, a person who sustains bodily injury or property damage in a motor vehicle accident may not recover non-economic damages from the at-fault owner or operator of another vehicle involved in the accident or from the at-fault parties insurer if, at the time of the accident, they were an uninsured motorist with a previous violation, defined as owning a motor vehicle without required financial responsibility and having been required to provide proof of future financial responsibility within the preceding five years, unless an exception applies.

Non-economic damages include compensation for physical and emotional pain and suffering, emotional distress, loss of enjoyment, and other similar intangible harms cited in Indiana Code § 34-30-29.2-2 and Indiana Code § 27-7-5.1-3. However, these statutes do not bar recovery of economic damages, such as medical expenses.

The No-Pay, No-Play restriction applies only to drivers who were uninsured at the time of the accident and who had a prior violation, such as a previous conviction for operating a vehicle without financial responsibility. When those criteria are met, the statute bars such individuals from recovering noneconomic damages, ensuring they do not receive a large personal injury settlement despite flouting mandatory insurance laws. The statutes are designed to penalize habitual noncompliance, not one-time lapses or situations where the driver is not legally responsible for insuring the vehicle.

Such laws can benefit an at-fault driver by preventing their auto insurance company from having to pay non-economic damages to an injured person—even when that injured person was not at fault for the accident.

I handled a personal injury case in which the No-Pay, No-Play laws became an issue. Defense counsel argued that my client was only entitled to compensation for his medical bills because he was driving uninsured when the collision occurred. However, I contended that the No-Pay, No-Play laws did not apply in this situation because my client was not the owner of the vehicle he was driving. Therefore, he did not meet the definition of an uninsured motorist with a previous violation, as outlined in Indiana Code § 27-7-5.1-4. According to the statute, the driver must own the uninsured vehicle involved in the accident for the No-Pay, No-Play rule to apply. A second exception, found in Indiana Code § 27-7-5.1-6, was also relevant to my case. In this instance, the defendant who struck my client was convicted of a crime in connection with the accident, which also rendered the No-Pay, No-Play law inapplicable. For these two reasons, I argued that the No-Pay, No-Play restrictions did not apply to my client's claim. I explained both points to defense counsel, but he continued to stall the case. Eventually, I filed a motion asking the court to rule on the legal issue. Shortly after the hearing was scheduled by the Court, the defense attorney made a reasonable offer, and the case settled.

In Indiana, uninsured drivers with a prior violation of the state's financial responsibility laws who are injured in an accident through no fault of their own may still recover economic damages, such as medical expenses and lost wages. However, they are barred from recovering non-economic damages, including pain and suffering, emotional distress, physical impairment, mental anguish, loss of enjoyment of life, and loss of companionship. The law provides limited exceptions, such as when the injured driver is under 18 years old or when the at-fault driver committed a crime in connection with the accident.

PERMISSIVE USER

As a personal injury attorney, you should also understand the term permissive user. When a person purchases car insurance, it is the vehicle itself that is insured. If you allow a friend to drive your car and they get into an accident, your friend—the permissive user—should be covered because the insurance follows the car, not the driver. Indiana courts have been liberal in defining who qualifies as a permissive user. In Indiana, express permission is not required; consent to use a vehicle may be implied from the circumstances of the case. However, an auto insurance policy may contain an exclusion clause. For example, if you have a teenage driver in your household, your policy may have an exclusion clause stating that the teenager is not permitted to drive your vehicle.

Indiana Code § 27-1-13-7 requires insurance companies to cover permissive users. The statute states permissive use of a vehicle may be expressed or implied by the owner. States often require auto insurance companies to cover permissive users for public policy reasons, to ensure there's financial resources available to compensate people injured by negligent drivers.

MINIMUM INSURANCE REQUIREMENTS

The State of Indiana requires all motorists to carry minimum liability insurance coverage, as set forth by statute. The minimum required limits are $25,000 in liability coverage for bodily injury or death to one person, $50,000 in total coverage for bodily injury or death to two or more people in a single accident, and $25,000 for property damage per accident. These minimums are commonly represented on an insurance policy as 25/50/25. Indiana Code § 9-25-4-5 sets forth the state's minimum liability insurance requirements for motorists.

SUMMARY OF THE LISA SAMPSON CASE FOR MODULE 3

After the collision, our legal team reviewed the crash report to evaluate liability. The report stated that Snake Jailbreak failed to obey a red traffic signal and entered the intersection while Lisa had the right of way. We also contacted the bystander witness identified in the crash report, who provided a recorded statement corroborating the account of the accident.

Regarding insurance coverage, Snake was driving a vehicle owned by his passenger, Liv Bouvier, at the time of the crash. Snake was a permissive user of Liv's vehicle. The crash report identified Unique Insurance as the auto insurer for Liv's vehicle. During the pre-suit investigation, the assigned adjuster from Unique Insurance confirmed that Liv carried the minimum liability limits required by Indiana law, which was $25,000.

END OF MODULE 3

This concludes Module 3. In Module 4, we will discuss damages.

DAMAGES

INTRODUCTION TO MODULE 4

For Module 4, we will address the topic of damages.

CATEGORIES OF DAMAGES

In an Indiana personal injury case, a plaintiff may seek compensation for several categories of damages. For example, in one of Morgan & Morgan's Indiana auto accident complaints, the following damages were listed: "past and future medical bills and related expense, lost income, lost future capacity to earn money, and past and future pain and suffering, both physical and mental." These categories of damages are included in the complaint's prayer for relief when filing a lawsuit.

ECONOMIC DAMAGES

Economic damages are meant to compensate for the financial losses resulting from injuries. Examples of economic damages include medical expenses, lost income, and property damage.

With respect to medical expenses, your client is entitled to reimbursement for reasonable and necessary costs, including future medical care. Recoverable expenses may include hospital stays, emergency room visits, physical therapy sessions, surgeries, prescription medications, and even the cost of traveling to and from medical facilities.

The other primary category of economic damages is lost income. Your client is entitled to reimbursement for any income lost as a result of the injury. For example, if your client was unable to work for three weeks due to a back injury from a car accident caused by another driver, he is entitled to the wages he would have earned during that time. Likewise, if the injury results in a disability that diminishes his future earning capacity, he is entitled to compensation for that future economic loss.

Kentucky attorney Michael Schafer wrote an excellent personal injury book that I keep in my library, titled *The Kentucky Accident Book: 7 Potholes That Can Wreck Your Kentucky Accident Case*. One section of the book I want to highlight is the author's discussion on developing lost wage claims. Schafer wrote:

> All lost wages need to be documented. First, your doctor needs to take you off work by stating that your injuries from the accident are preventing you from doing your job for a period of time—that if you work, it will interfere with your recovery. If you don't have this, it is very difficult, if not impossible, to collect on your lost wage claim. Second, you need to inform your employer that you were in an automobile accident and that you can't work. This way, your personnel file will be properly documented.

Attorney Steven Burris, in *Automobile Accident Cases in Las Vegas*, also emphasized the importance of providing complete wage documentation to the liability insurer when pursuing a lost wage claim. He wrote:

> As far as lost wages go, insurance companies believe we are still in the 1950's, where if you miss a day of work you need a doctor's excuse, much like getting a parent's excuse for missing a day of school. If you do not have the excuse from the doctor then they do not count the day of lost wages."

Economic damages also include compensation for property damage, such as damage to your client's vehicle or other personal property. When a vehicle is totaled, the appropriate measure of damages is its fair market value immediately before the accident. If the vehicle is damaged but not totaled, the primary measure of damages is the reduction in its fair market value caused by the tortfeasor's negligence. The cost of repairs may be used to calculate damages if the repairs fully restore the vehicle to its pre-accident condition. However, if repairs alone cannot restore the vehicle's original value—such as in the case of classic vehicles—the diminished value must be demonstrated through additional evidence. This may include appraisals, market valuation reports, expert assessments, and comparable sales data. Presenting such evidence to the insurance adjuster helps substantiate the claim for compensation beyond the cost of repairs.

NON-ECONOMIC DAMAGES

Economic damages are essential to a personal injury claim, but the significant compensation in large cases often lies in non-economic damages.

Non-economic damages are designed to compensate your client for the non-monetary impact of their injury. These damages refer to compensation for subjective losses, such as pain and suffering, emotional distress, loss of enjoyment of life, and loss of consortium. While your client is entitled to reimbursement for medical expenses, those expenses do not account for the pain and suffering caused by the injury itself. Damages for pain and suffering specifically include compensation for having to endure physical pain and discomfort that your client would not have experienced but for the accident.

Emotional distress includes psychological effects such as anxiety, depression, panic attacks, sleep disorders, and post-traumatic stress disorder (PTSD), all stemming directly from the accident and its aftermath. The most compelling evidence of emotional distress is documentation by a physician in the medical records. For example, if your client has seen a therapist, counselor, or psychiatrist since the accident, any new diagnosis or change in medication may serve as evidence supporting the claim for emotional distress.

Non-economic damages may also include loss of enjoyment of life, which refers to a diminished ability to engage in activities and experiences the injured party once enjoyed. This includes hobbies, exercise, social interactions, and general day-to-day pleasures that are now limited due to the injury.

Finally, if your client was married at the time of the accident, their spouse may pursue compensation for loss of consortium. This refers to the loss of companionship, affection, support, and intimacy resulting from the injuries. Loss of consortium claims are typically reserved for cases involving severe injuries or death.

PUNITIVE DAMAGES

Punitive damages are distinct from economic and non-economic damages; they are intended to punish defendants for especially egregious misconduct and to deter similar behavior in others. These damages are typically awarded only when the defendant's conduct is found to be malicious, willful, wanton, or grossly negligent. However, most insurance policies exclude coverage for punitive damages. As a result, if punitive damages are awarded, the plaintiff must collect them directly from the defendant.

Indiana law imposes specific limitations on punitive damages. Under Indiana Code § 34-51-3-4, a punitive damages award may not exceed the greater of (1) three times the amount of compensatory damages awarded or (2) $50,000. In other words, the cap is whichever of these two figures results in a higher amount.

For example, if a plaintiff is awarded $10,000 in compensatory damages, three times that amount would be $30,000. Because $50,000 is greater than $30,000, the maximum punitive damages that could be awarded in that case would be $50,000. On the other hand, if the plaintiff is awarded $100,000 in compensatory damages, the cap would be $300,000 (three times the compensatory award), because that amount is greater than $50,000.

Compensatory damages include both economic damages (such as medical bills and lost wages) and non-economic damages (such as pain and suffering or emotional distress). The cap applies to punitive damages only and does not limit the amount of compensatory damages a plaintiff can recover.

Even if punitive damages are awarded and successfully collected from the defendant, the plaintiff is not entitled to the full amount. Under Indiana Code § 34-51-3-6, only 25% of a punitive damages award is paid to the plaintiff. The remaining 75% must be transferred to the Indiana State Treasurer, who deposits the funds into the Violent Crime Victim's Compensation Fund.

VALUING CASES

In his book *Winning Personal Injury Cases*, Attorney Evan Aidman provides practical guidance on evaluating damages in personal injury claims. In the chapter titled "Damages," Aidman offers readers useful rough estimates of case values based on the nature and severity of the injuries involved.

For smaller cases, Aidman emphasizes that the two primary factors influencing settlement value are the duration of treatment and the amount of medical expenses incurred. He wrote, "for simple cases, such as neck and back sprains (soft tissue injuries), the key factors are length of treatment and the amount of the medical bills." He continued, "perhaps one rule of thumb for soft tissue injury cases is $1,500-$2,000 for each month of treatment. Thus, a soft tissue back and neck injury with three months of treatment would probably settle for between $4,500 and $6,000."

When discussing more serious injuries, such as ruptured discs, bone fractures, or injuries resulting in visible scarring, Aidman notes that these conditions are easier to prove and typically command higher settlement values from insurance carriers.

On valuing herniated disc cases, he offers the following analysis:

"In an urban area, a 20-year-old who suffers a herniated lumbar disc that does not compress the nerves and does not require surgery is likely to obtain a settlement between $30,000 and $50,000. In a less urban area, the settlement could range from $20,000 to $40,000.

If the herniated disc compresses the nerve roots, this adds value to the case, as it indicates the plaintiff is in considerable pain. A rough estimate would be that the herniated disc with compression is worth at least $10,000 more than a disc that does not compress the nerve roots."

Aidman further explains that surgical removal of a herniation can increase a case's value by an additional $40,000 or more, and that if further surgeries are needed, the valuation can increase even more.

Concerning catastrophic injuries, Aidman observes that, "the largest jury awards and settlements involve severe head injuries, loss of limbs, paralysis, eye injuries, and death." He adds, "insurance claims adjusters fear huge jury verdicts on cases involving severe, permanent injury—especially if they respect the plaintiff's lawyer."

Attorney Steven Burris, in *Automobile Accident Cases in Las Vegas*, also gave some real-life insight on how insurance companies value cases. Burris wrote, "The current experience of my office (this in in 2018) is that, in Las Vegas, at least, the adjuster on auto cases will typically start out at medical bills (per the calculation of what is 'fair' for them), plus about $1,500 a month for pain and suffering. On MIST (minor impact) cases, typically the first offers are less—less than the medical bills, not uncommonly."

Burris also gave insights on how much you can expect an offer to increase in pre-litigation following the first offer. Burris wrote, "My own experience is that typically, the pre-litigation adjusters (at least, the ones not trying to be 'heroes') will go up about 15% above their first offers, and if that is insufficient, then they really don't care, because now the case will shift to the 'litigation adjuster,' the next step up the ladder."

> ### 💡 PRACTICE TIP: Associate with a Trial Lawyer
>
> If you are not a trial lawyer and take on a case involving severe injuries, associating a respected trial attorney can significantly enhance the case's value.

USING ITEMIZATION TO PRESENT DAMAGES

I once sat second chair in a trial where the lead attorney, a seasoned litigator, used a technique called itemization in his closing argument. Standing before the jury, he methodically listed past medical bills, future medical expenses, and pain and suffering on a giant notepad, assigning a specific dollar value to each category. Because the plaintiff did not work, he excluded lost wages and loss of future earning capacity. He then totaled the amounts—which exceeded $100,000—providing the jury with a clear, structured rationale for the requested compensation. This approach not only simplified the damages calculation but also reinforced the fairness of the award. You can apply the same technique in your demand letters to illustrate your client's losses in a compelling, logical way.

> ### 💡 PRACTICE TIP: Tell the Jury What You Want
>
> Top personal injury trial attorney Mike Rafi once advised in a YouTube video that trial lawyers should present their requested damages award to the jury at multiple stages of the trial. He emphasized the importance of referencing the specific amount during voir dire, the opening statement, and the closing argument to reinforce the claim. By consistently presenting the damages figure, he believed the jury would develop a stronger understanding of the plaintiff's desired outcome and be more inclined to award the full amount sought.

THE HUMAN ELEMENT

One of the top trucking accident attorneys in the United States is Joseph Fried. In one of his presentations on damages, he emphasized the critical importance of incorporating the plaintiff's human story into the case. I must stress that this is very important. In a case I handled while working at Isaacs & Isaacs, the pre-litigation attorney was unable to secure a reasonable offer from the insurance company, so the case was forwarded to the litigation department and assigned to me. Before filing a lawsuit, I crafted a new demand letter seeking policy limits. In that demand letter, I highlighted how the accident had impacted my client's ability to care for her special needs son. After sending the new demand letter to the adjuster, I quickly received a call offering to settle for the policy limits. By emphasizing the human element of the personal injury claim, the pre-litigation offer jumped from $8,000 to the $25,000 policy limit. This experience reinforced for me the importance of conveying the human aspects of a case to an adjuster, rather than solely presenting medical bills and records and lost wage information.

Joseph Fried also stressed in his presentation the importance of utilizing "before-and-after witnesses." In one of my cases, I implemented this strategy by contacting several of my client's family members and friends, recording their statements describing how healthy my client was before being hit by a car, and detailing how severely impaired he was afterward. I then provided these recorded statements to both the adjuster and, later, the mediator.

Fried further emphasized that damages drive the value of a case more than liability. Therefore, to obtain a substantial settlement or jury award, you must focus on developing the damages. One specific technique Fried suggested to strengthen damages is to include a well-documented lost wage claim in the demand packet. I must emphasize that developing a lost wage claim requires diligent work—substantial documentation must be provided to the adjuster to verify the claim. Without it, the adjuster will likely omit lost wages from their settlement evaluation. According to Fried, presenting a complete picture of both the medical and lost wage aspects of your client's case leads to a significantly enhanced case valuation.

THE COLLATERAL SOURCE RULE

In Indiana, when a driver's negligence causes injury to another person, the at-fault driver must pay for the injured person's reasonable and necessary medical expenses. One common way to prove that medical expenses are reasonable is to present the medical provider's statement of charges for treatment related to the accident. Under Indiana Evidence Rule 413, such statements are admissible in court and serve as prima facie evidence that the charges are reasonable.

The collateral source rule itself has deep historical roots. In 1854, the United States Supreme Court first announced what is now known as the "collateral source rule." Under this rule, a defendant must bear the full cost of the injury they caused the plaintiff, regardless of any compensation the plaintiff receives from an independent or "collateral" source. Prior to 1986, Indiana followed this traditional common law approach, which barred defendants from introducing evidence of compensation the plaintiff received from sources other than the defendant or the defendant's insurer. This rule was intended to prevent tortfeasors from benefiting from payments made to the plaintiff by independent third parties.

However, in 1986, Indiana enacted legislation that significantly modified this doctrine. Under the current statutory framework, defendants may present evidence at trial of collateral source payments the plaintiff has received. In *How to Successfully Litigate a Personal Injury Case*, Attorney Andrew Smiley explained: "The term 'collateral source' refers to benefits that your client may be receiving as a result of an injury from an accident. Medicare, Medicaid, Workers' Compensation, and disability benefits are all collateral sources. It is a source of something benefiting the client that is collateral to the case because it is outside the case."

The purpose of Indiana's collateral source statute is to prevent plaintiffs from receiving an excessive recovery that exceeds their actual monetary loss resulting from a personal injury. The statute aims to ensure that compensation reflects the true economic harm suffered.

A key case interpreting Indiana's collateral source statute is *Stanley v. Walker, 906 N.E.2d 852 (Ind. 2009)*, authored by Indiana Supreme Court Justice Frank Sullivan. (Fun fact: Justice Sullivan instructed me in two law school courses, and I earned an A in one of them.) The decision established what is now commonly referred to as the Stanley doctrine, which clarified how the collateral source statute applies in personal injury litigation.

In *Stanley v. Walker*, the Indiana Supreme Court held that a defendant in a personal injury action may introduce evidence of discounted medical payments negotiated between the plaintiff's medical providers and their health insurance company to prove the reasonable value of medical services. The Court determined that the reasonable value of medical treatment is not necessarily limited to either the billed amount or the amount paid after negotiated discounts—it could be either, or even somewhere in between. The Court wrote, "In sum, the proper measure of medical expenses in Indiana is the reasonable value of such expenses. This measure of damages cannot be read as permitting only full recovery of medical expenses billed to a plaintiff. Nor can the proper measure of medical expenses be read as permitting only the recovery of the amount actually paid. The focus is on the reasonable value, not the actual charge."

The Court explained that evidence of reduced payments accepted as full satisfaction for medical services is relevant to determining the reasonableness of claimed medical expenses. Therefore, such evidence is admissible under Indiana law to assist the jury in evaluating the proper amount of damages.

Ultimately, the Court concluded that a jury may consider two key figures when assessing the reasonable value of medical expenses incurred by a plaintiff: (1) the total amount billed by the healthcare provider for services rendered; and (2) the reduced amount accepted by the provider as full payment. This ruling empowers juries to weigh both amounts to arrive at a fair and accurate award for medical expenses.

THE JURY'S ROLE IN VALUING DAMAGES

In conclusion, a plaintiff may introduce medical bills as evidence to support a claim for damages related to medical treatment. In turn, the defendant may present evidence of discounts—such as write-downs or write-offs—to challenge or provide context for the claimed value of those services. Ultimately, it is the jury's responsibility to weigh all of the evidence and determine the reasonable value of the medical expenses.

SUMMARY OF LISA SAMPSON'S CASE FOR MODULE 4

Lisa Sampson's damages resulting from the auto accident fall into both economic and non-economic categories. Her economic damages include past medical expenses, lost wages, and property damage. Lisa received treatment for soft tissue injuries over a span of a few months, which included emergency care, diagnostic imaging, and physical therapy. Her medical expenses were initially paid in part by her MedPay policy, which provided $5,000 in coverage. Once that amount was exhausted, her health insurer, Anthem, covered most of her medical bills.

Regarding Lisa's lost income damages, her treating physician issued a written work restriction, which we submitted to the liability insurance adjuster as part of the demand packet along with a wage and salary verification form completed by her employer, Home Depot. The wage and salary verification form—commonly used in personal injury cases—provides a straightforward way for employers to confirm the specific days or hours of work missed and the corresponding wages lost due to accident-related injuries. Although Lisa's tax statements were later produced in response to the defendant's Request for Production during discovery, they were not included in the demand packet. Because Lisa missed only a few days of work, her annual tax returns would not have reflected a measurable loss of income, making them an ineffective tool for proving damages at the pre-litigation stage.

Lisa Sampson's non-economic damages, as reflected in her medical records, include right hip pain, bruising to her right thigh, neck and back pain, left wrist pain, sleep disruption, and reduced participation in daily activities. Throughout her treatment, Lisa consistently reported physical pain and discomfort, which is documented in provider notes and supports a general claim for pain and suffering. In addition, her records reflect difficulty sleeping and elevated stress levels following the accident, illustrating the broader impact the collision had on her daily functioning. Lisa also reported a temporary inability to engage in social outings and recreational activities she previously enjoyed. These limitations, noted during medical visits, demonstrate a diminished quality of life during her recovery and further support her claim for non-economic damages.

END OF MODULE 4

This concludes Module 4 on damages. In Module 5, we will turn our attention to the demand packet.

THE DEMAND PACKET

INTRODUCTION TO DEMAND PACKETS

Now, let's talk about one of my favorite tasks as a personal injury attorney: creating and sending out the demand packet.

LISA'S POST-ACCIDENT MEDICAL TIMELINE

We will begin by providing a timeline of the medical providers Lisa went to following the car accident on June 1, 2024. After the wreck, the Yellow Ambulance Company promptly transported Lisa to Clark Memorial Hospital for evaluation. Upon arrival, she received x-rays, was prescribed crutches, and prescribed pain medication, which she picked up from Walgreens. Three days after the accident, on June 4, 2024, Lisa visited her primary care physician at Strickland, Cox, and Associates for further assessment. Following this appointment, Lisa was ordered to begin physical therapy at Chamber Medical Group, which commenced on June 4, 2024, and continued through October 4, 2024.

HIGHLIGHTING KEY MEDICAL RECORDS

Every personal injury attorney should thoroughly review their client's medical records and identify crucial details to later emphasize to the adjuster. For example, upon receiving Lisa's medical records, I noted that the ambulance report stated Lisa's vehicle was propelled approximately 30 yards down the road, and she was vocal about experiencing severe hip pain immediately after the accident.

Upon arriving at the hospital, she underwent X-rays while continually reporting hip pain.

At the hospital, Lisa was prescribed crutches supplied by the medical equipment company Bregs, Inc. That same day, she was also prescribed muscle relaxers and pain relievers. On June 4, 2024, Lisa visited her primary care physician at Strickland, Cox, and Associates, reporting ongoing back pain that had not improved since the accident. She also began physical therapy at Chambers Medical Group on that same day after the therapy was ordered by her primary care physician. A medical note from three months after the accident, in September, indicated that Lisa was still experiencing significant pain, which was attributed to the car wreck.

CALCULATING MEDICAL BILLS

Below are the medical bill totals from the various providers Lisa saw due to injuries from the accident.

- ► Yellow Ambulance Company of Southern Indiana: $1,000
- ► Clark Memorial Hospital: $2,500
- ► Radiology Associates: $400
- ► Breg, Inc.: $300
- ► Walgreens: $100
- ► Strickland, Cox, & Associates: $200
- ► Chambers Medical Group: $8,500

The total amount of these medical bills is $13,000. These charges are commonly referred to as medical special damages, or simply "specials." Specials represent the total amount billed by medical providers for accident-related treatment, before any payments by health insurance, write-offs, or negotiated reductions. Plaintiffs' attorneys often emphasize this figure in demand letters to illustrate the full extent of the client's medical expenses.

However, the actual amount Lisa owes after med-pay coverage, health insurance payments, write-offs, and lien reductions is much less than the billed total. You will see this difference in Module 9, when we discuss the settlement.

DETAILED DEMAND LETTERS

Many law firms and attorneys rely on standardized demand letters; however, I personally crafted a tailored demand letter for each personal injury claim I managed, considering this best practice. This individualized approach is adopted by leading trial attorneys nationwide. For instance, a demand letter I reviewed online prepared by prominent Maryland personal injury attorney Ronald V. Miller, Jr. demanded $100,000 for his client, clearly outlined the defendant's liability, and meticulously detailed the plaintiff's injuries and medical treatments. The letter noted medical expenses totaling $18,350, supported by attached bills and records. Additionally, Miller included a lost wage verification signed by the plaintiff's employer and a signed statement from her financial planner, as well as documentation of her miscellaneous out-of-pocket expenses. For those seeking to learn more about Miller's approach, his law firm's website offers a comprehensive collection of personal injury forms and sample documents for attorneys to study. These resources are available at https://www.millerandzois.com/professional-attorney-information-center/.

For Lisa Sampson's demand letter, I highlighted multiple key points to bolster her case with the liability adjuster. To review Lisa's demand letter, refer to Exhibit 5.

When our law firm sent out the demand letter we also included several attachments which aren't shown in Exhibit 5. Lisa's demand packet included her medical records and bills, photos of her bruising and vehicle, video and aerial photos of the accident scene and vehicle paths, and a probable cause affidavit from the defendant's related criminal case. The affidavit detailed how the defendant was drinking and driving, and fled the scene after striking Lisa. The packet also included the defendant's rap sheet, which showed his extensive criminal history. After reviewing the letter and its attachments, I believe the insurance adjuster will find this case particularly memorable, especially when compared to others in which counsels failed to provide such a comprehensive and well-documented packet.

You should include a variety of supporting documentation with your demand packet to strengthen your claim. Any evidence that strengthens the case for liability or underscores the severity of your client's damages is highly valuable. For example, if your client has a visible scar resulting from the accident, take a clear photograph and include it, as scarring can significantly increase the value of the claim. Similarly, if you have a sworn statement from an eyewitness, include that as well. In his book *Winning Personal Injury Cases*, Attorney Evan Aidman stated he will also sometimes put e-mails clients send him directly into the settlement demand. Such an act further humanizes the claim. The more compelling and well-documented your demand packet is, the more persuasive it will be during settlement negotiations.

EFFECTIVE DEMAND LETTER STRATEGIES

Mike Rafi is one of the leading personal injury and trial attorneys in America. He maintains a comprehensive collection of educational videos on YouTube, where he discusses various aspects of personal injury law. In one of his videos, Rafi explains his approach to sending out demand packets. He typically includes a deadline for the adjuster to respond and ensures that the amount he demands falls within the policy limits. He also warns the insurance company that failure to settle could expose their insured's personal assets if a jury verdict exceeds those limits.

Additionally, Rafi may incorporate specific excerpts from medical records or deposition transcripts directly into the demand letter or include them as attachments. He also noted that he sends his demand letters via certified mail and stated that it is not uncommon for him to send more than ten demand letters in a single case, updating the insurer with each demand as more information becomes available.

DEVELOPING THE LOST WAGE CLAIM

To support your client's lost wage claim, you should submit a range of documentation to the insurance adjuster. This may include a wage and salary verification form to be completed by the client's employer, a leave of absence letter from the plaintiff's treating physician, relevant tax records, and recent pay stubs. You may also consider including job performance reviews or letters from the plaintiff's management team, which can emphasize how essential the plaintiff was to their business. These materials help build a strong foundation for proving wage loss and can improve your client's chances of receiving full compensation.

USING DRONE PHOTOS TO SHOW THE SCENE

In a demand packet to the adjuster, I recommend including an aerial photograph of the accident scene. You can enhance the image by inserting diagrams that show the positions of the vehicles involved in the collision. This type of visual aid can greatly assist the adjuster in understanding and visualizing how the accident occurred.

PLAINTIFF'S VEHICLE

Exhibit 6 contains a photograph of Lisa Sampson's vehicle, which was provided to the insurance adjuster during the claim process. However, it's important to recognize that such vehicle photos are not always helpful— especially when there is minimal visible damage—as they can undermine the perceived severity of the plaintiff's injuries.

IMPACTFUL USE OF INJURY VIDEO EVIDENCE

I once had a client who was severely injured after being struck by a car while walking through a parking lot, leaving him with a pronounced limp. After the case failed to settle during the pre-litigation phase, it was sent to the litigation department and assigned to me. Once I took over, I had the client come to the law office, and I used my GoPro to film him walking down the stairs to his car—capturing just how much the vehicle impact had physically affected him. I sent that video to defense counsel, who then used it to persuade the liability adjuster to settle the case for policy limits.

Seeing the client's limp on video–rather than merely reading about it–completely transformed the case's value with the liability insurer. What was once viewed as a minor claim valued at a few thousand dollars turned into a $25,000 policy limits offer.

The importance of this technique is echoed in *The Complete Personal Injury Practice Manual*, where the authors Al Cone and Verne Lawyer wrote:

> If the plaintiff has disfiguring injuries or other injuries which are readily observable, very often, his appearing at deposition time is a long stride towards serious settlement negotiations by the defendant's attorney. The defendant's attorney, the busy insurance lawyer, has many files in his office. And in most instances, the client's case does not really come alive to the defense lawyer until that lawyer sees the plaintiff. Usually, this is at discovery deposition time.

🔆 PRACTICE TIP: Admitting Visual Evidence at Trial

The book *The Complete Personal Injury Practice Manual* offers helpful guidance on how to lay a foundation for admitting picture and video evidence of your client's injuries at trial. The authors Al Cone and Verne Lawyer explain that if the plaintiff's attorney personally takes photos, the key to admissibility is having a witness—typically the client—testify that the picture is a fair and accurate portrayal of what it depicts. As they state: "If the plaintiff's lawyer acts as a cameraman and takes pictures for use at trial, the witness should be asked if the pictures are fair and accurate, and a portrayal of that which they are intended to portray. Invariably, the witness will admit that they are, and a foundation is laid for future admission at trial. This technique may also be used with the identification of other exhibits."

HANDLING PREEXISTING CONDITIONS

Now, let's discuss how to handle demands involving clients with preexisting injuries. If you anticipate that the adjuster will scrutinize the preexisting condition, it may be beneficial to obtain a narrative report or affidavit from your client's treating physician. This report should detail the nature of the preexisting condition, the new injuries sustained in the accident and their severity, how the accident exacerbated the preexisting condition, and the anticipated future treatment. It should also include an estimate of the cost of that future treatment.

Before requesting a narrative report, plaintiff's counsel should ensure the physician is fully informed about any relevant preexisting injuries or medical conditions. Counsel should provide the physician with a comprehensive overview of the plaintiff's medical history, including prior symptoms, the timing and nature of the last treatment for the condition before the accident, and any other pertinent details. Complete copies of the plaintiff's prior medical records should also be provided.

In the demand letter accompanying the narrative report, be sure to explain the eggshell-plaintiff principle and cite specific case law supporting it.

EVALUATING AND RESPONDING TO THE OFFER

In Lisa's case, we received a response from the adjuster regarding our demand letter. On October 18, 2024, we requested the $25,000 policy limit in our demand. On November 13, 2024, we received an initial offer from Unique Insurance in the amount of $14,300. This initial offer is not unreasonable, considering that Lisa's actual out-of-pocket medical expenses—after insurance payments, reductions, and write-offs—total only around $3,000, compared to the $13,000 originally billed by her providers. That said, it is important to remember that the insurance company's first offer is rarely its final one.

One potential strategy for increasing a settlement offer without filing suit is to contact the adjuster to discuss the factors influencing their valuation. For example, if the claim includes lost wages, inquire whether that evidence was considered in the initial offer—and if not, why. You can also ask whether any additional documentation would assist the adjuster in fully evaluating the claim.

BREAKING DOWN THE OFFER FOR THE CLIENT

One of my favorite tasks after receiving an insurance offer was calculating how much the firm and the client would receive under the proposed offer. Once you've done the math, you should call the client to discuss how much they would receive in their pocket based on the proposed settlement. During this conversation, advise the client on whether you believe they should accept the offer and, if not, outline the next strategic step. Ultimately, the decision to accept a settlement rests with the client, but it is your role to provide clear, informed guidance.

HOW TO PRESSURE THE ADJUSTER AND DEFENSE

Below, I provided a list of strategies to help apply pressure on the adjuster and defense counsel to encourage settlement. Creating pressure on these parties can help foster an environment more conducive to resolution.

First, you can pressure the adjuster by submitting a comprehensive and well-organized demand packet that justifies a fair payout. When the adjuster has all necessary documentation and receives a reasonable settlement offer, they are more likely to feel compelled to resolve the case.

Another effective method is to arrange a direct conversation with the adjuster, typically by phone, to apply verbal pressure.

You can also schedule depositions, which may increase the insurer's litigation costs, creating financial pressure. The act also requires defense counsel to work harder, which may incentivize them to work toward a settlement.

Further, scheduling a trial date with the court signals that you are serious about litigating the case, which can pressure both the adjuster and defense counsel to move toward settlement. At my former employer, one of our top trial attorneys made it a priority to secure a trial date shortly after filing suit—a tactic intended to put immediate pressure on defense counsel.

I also personally focused on maintaining momentum in my assigned cases. To keep the defense moving, I promptly responded to discovery requests and immediately served my own discovery requests upon defense counsel's appearance in the case.

You can further strengthen your settlement position by providing defense counsel with relevant jury verdict information and pairing it with a reasonable settlement offer. Together, these materials can help defense counsel persuade the adjuster of the benefits of resolving the case before trial.

PRESSURING THE DEFENDANT

You can apply pressure directly on the defendant by making them aware that, if the insurance company fails to settle the case and it proceeds to trial, any verdict exceeding the policy limits could result in them having personal liability for the excess amount. This information can be communicated through a letter to the defendant's attorney or during the defendant's deposition. Doing so puts the defendant on notice of their potential individual exposure, which can lead them to pressure their insurer to settle the claim in order to avoid personal financial risk.

UTILIZING BAD FAITH LAW TO YOUR ADVANTAGE

In tort cases, there is no fiduciary relationship between the tortfeasor's liability insurer and the claimant, even if the same insurer insures both the plaintiff and defendant. However, when representing a client in an underinsured or uninsured motorist claim against their own auto insurer, it is essential to understand Indiana's Unfair Claim Settlement Practices Act (Indiana Code § 27-4-1 et. seq.). This law establishes an implied duty of good faith and fair dealing in all insurance contracts.

Under this duty, insurers are obligated to act in good faith toward their insureds and may be held liable in tort for bad faith claim handling. This includes refraining from unjustified refusals to pay policy benefits, causing unreasonable delays in payment, misleading the insured, or using unfair tactics to pressure the insured into settling.

If your client believes they have been subjected to an unfair claims settlement practice, they may file a complaint with the Indiana Insurance Commissioner. Filing such a complaint can prompt the insurer to take the claim more seriously and may help generate a more reasonable settlement offer.

SUMMARY OF LISA SAMPSON'S CASE FOR MODULE 5

After Lisa Sampson completed her medical treatment, our legal team assembled a compelling demand packet to begin settlement negotiations with the liability insurer, Unique Insurance. The medical documentation in the packet starts with the June 1, 2024, ambulance report. Lisa was transported by Yellow Ambulance Company to Clark Memorial Hospital. The ambulance report clearly states that the other vehicle ran a red light and struck Lisa's car on the passenger side, pushing it 30 yards down the street. The report also documents Lisa's complaint of severe right hip pain at the scene.

At Clark Memorial Hospital, Lisa reported pain in her right hip, wrist, and back. Following a medical examination, x-rays were taken. After confirming that Lisa had no fractures or other serious injuries, she was discharged with crutches and prescriptions for a muscle relaxer and pain medication, both of which pharmacy records show were promptly filled.

On June 4, 2024, Lisa followed up with her primary care physician at Strickland, Cox, and Associates and reported persistent back pain from the crash, stating that the pain had not improved. That same day, she began a course of physical therapy at Chambers Medical Group, a clinic specializing in the treatment of auto accident victims. Her initial consultation there noted pain in her hip, mid and low back, bruising on her legs and back, and pain radiating down her right leg. She also reported headaches, neck pain, and difficulty sleeping.

According to her medical records from a visit to Chambers Medical Group on June 8, 2024, Lisa was officially diagnosed with muscle strains in her neck, upper back, and lower back, as well as a sprain in her hip area. Her medical records indicated that her past medical history was noncontributory and that her hip and back pain began immediately after the accident. The records further noted that therapy appointments occasionally caused her to be late to work, illustrating the impact of her injuries on daily functioning. A medical note from September 2024 confirmed that Lisa continued to suffer significant pain months after the crash.

Lisa continued treatment at Chambers Medical Group through October 4, 2024, incurring total medical charges of $8,500. After payments from her MedPay coverage and health insurance, her remaining out-of-pocket responsibility to Chambers was $2,500. This reduced amount reflects her actual financial liability after insurance contributions and provider write-offs.

These medical records and billing statements were reviewed in detail and included in the demand packet. The demand letter emphasized Lisa's extensive therapy treatment, the human impact of her injuries—including the interruption of her college career—and the seriousness of the crash itself. The supporting materials included her medical records, medical bills, lost wage documentation, photographs of Lisa, her vehicle, and the accident scene, video of the vehicle paths, a probable cause affidavit from the criminal case against the defendant, Snake Jailbreak, and documentation of his extensive criminal history.

The demand letter requested the full $25,000 policy limits. Our legal team submitted the demand packet to Unique Insurance on October 18, 2024. On November 13, 2024, the insurer responded with an initial offer of $14,300. We advised Lisas on the pros and cons of accepting the offer, clearly explaining how much she would net and whether further negotiations or litigation might yield a better result. Ultimately, after discussion Lisa decided to deny the initial offer of $14,300 and move forward with pursuing the full $25,000 policy. Our firm then called the adjuster and alerted him that the offer was denied, and we wouldn't be settling for anything less than the full policy.

END OF MODULE 5

This concludes Module 5. In Module 6, we will cover medical liens and their impact on personal injury cases.

LIENS

INTRODUCTION TO LIENS IN PERSONAL INJURY CASES

Liens commonly arise in personal injury cases. This typically occurs when medical care providers seek reimbursement for services rendered, or when health insurance companies attempt to recoup the medical expenses they paid on the client's behalf from any future settlement. Such liens ensure that medical providers or insurers are compensated before any settlement proceeds are distributed to the client.

SUBROGATION LIENS

In personal injury cases, both a plaintiff's MedPay lien through their auto insurance company and a health insurance company lien are commonly referred to as subrogation liens. A subrogation lien allows your client's health insurer or auto insurer providing MedPay benefits to assert a right of reimbursement from the proceeds of a personal injury settlement for medical expenses paid on the client's behalf. When an auto insurance company pays for a plaintiff's medical expenses under MedPay coverage, it may seek reimbursement from the settlement proceeds. A MedPay lien is considered a form of subrogation because the insurer is asserting the plaintiff's right to recover those expenses from the at-fault party. Similarly, when a health insurance company pays for treatment related to the injury, it may assert a subrogation claim against any recovery the plaintiff receives from the liable third party.

Indiana attorneys frequently use statutory law to reduce the impact of subrogation liens on their clients' settlements. In a CLE discussion about liens, Indiana personal injury attorney Ted Smith explained, "Indiana has two statutes which may diminish or reduce subrogation liens. The first is Indiana Code § 34-53-1-2. This statute deals with the reduction of a subrogation lien by the pro rata share of attorney fees and costs of litigation. The second is Indiana Code § 34-51-2-19. This statute mandates the reduction of a subrogation lien due to the comparative fault of the insured or by reason of uncollectibility. These two statutes are used often by Indiana attorneys to help maximize the recovery for their clients in personal injury cases."

REDUCING SUBROGATION LIENS: INDIANA CODE § 34-53-1-2 (COMMON FUND DOCTRINE)

One statute that can reduce or diminish a subrogation lien is Indiana Code § 34-53-1-2, which codifies the common fund doctrine. This doctrine recognizes that it is the plaintiff's attorney who secures the settlement, which ultimately benefits the insurer by enabling reimbursement of medical expenses. Consequently, the plaintiff's insurer should contribute to the legal fees since it benefits financially from the attorney's efforts. Under the common fund doctrine, the insurer is required to pay its fair share of the attorney's fees and litigation costs incurred in obtaining the settlement.

APPLICATION OF THE COMMON FUND DOCTRINE

Here is an example of how the common fund doctrine works. Sally settles her car accident case for $25,000. Her attorney advanced $1,250 in deposition cost to recover the $25,000. Sally agreed to pay her attorney a one-third (33 1/3) percent contingency fee. The total attorney's fees would be $8,333.33. Sally's health insurance company paid Sally's medical providers $4,000 for Sally's medical treatment that resulted from the car accident. In this case, Sally's health insurance company must reduce the amount owed by 38% because that is the pro-rata share of attorney fees, and deposition costs ($8,333.33+$1,250/$25,000 = 38%). So, the amount owed by Sally to her Health Insurance Company who holds the lien is $2,480. [$4,000-($4,000*0.38)=2,480]. So after the reduction due to the Common Fund Doctrine the lien is now $2,480 versus the original $4,000 lien amount.

REDUCING SUBROGATION LIENS: INDIANA CODE § 34-51-2-19 (LIEN REDUCTION STATUTE)

The second statute that attorney Ted Smith mentioned, which can reduce or diminish a subrogation lien, is Indiana Code § 34-51-2-19, commonly referred to as the lien reduction statute. This statute governs the reduction of liens related to medical expenses in personal injury cases and identifies two scenarios in which a client's insurance lien may be reduced.

First, if the plaintiff is found to be partially at fault for their injuries, the insurance company is required to proportionately reduce its medical payment subrogation lien.

Second, a lien may be reduced due to the uncollectibility of the full value of the claim. This typically arises when the reasonable value of the plaintiff's personal injury claim exceeds the defendant's available insurance policy limits.

Additionally, the lien reduction statute provides that the party asserting the lien must bear its pro rata share of the plaintiff's attorney's fees and litigation expenses.

APPLICATION OF THE LIEN REDUCTION STATUTE

Let's look at a practical illustration of how Indiana's lien reduction statute can operate in real life. Suppose the plaintiff recovers $100,000, which represents the full amount available under the defendant's insurance policy. However, the plaintiff's claim is reasonably valued at $500,000. In this situation, the plaintiff's attorney could argue that the subrogation lien should be reduced proportionally—by 80%—to reflect the uncollectibility of the full value of the claim.

The rationale behind this approach is that it would be unfair for a lienholder to recover the full amount of its lien when the plaintiff is only receiving a small portion of their actual damages. By invoking the lien reduction statute, the attorney ensures that the available recovery is distributed more equitably rather than allowing the lienholder to consume a disproportionate share of the settlement.

HOSPITAL LIENS

A hospital lien is a statutory claim that enables a hospital to recover the reasonable value of medical services provided to a patient injured due to the negligence of a third party. Indiana's Hospital Lien Statute, codified at IC 32-33-4 et seq., safeguards the financial interests of hospitals treating patients for accident-related injuries. When a patient receives treatment following an accident, the hospital may seek reimbursement for the cost of care by asserting a lien against any personal injury settlement or judgment the patient obtains from the at-fault party. The lien attaches to the portion of the recovery attributable to the hospital's charges. However, the statute balances the hospital's right to reimbursement with the interests of the injured party and their legal counsel, explicitly providing that a perfected hospital lien is subordinate to all reasonable claims for attorney's fees, court costs, and other litigation-related expenses. This ensures that the patient's ability to secure legal representation and pursue fair compensation is not compromised by an overwhelming lien.

To enforce a hospital lien in Indiana, strict statutory procedures must be followed. The hospital must perfect its lien by completing two steps. First, within 90 days after the patient's discharge or before final settlement of the claim (whichever occurs first), the hospital must file a verified statement in writing with the recorder's office in the county where the hospital is located. This verified statement must include the patient's name and address, the hospital's name and address, the dates of treatment, the amount claimed to be due for services, and the names and addresses of all persons or entities alleged to be liable for the injuries. Second, within 10 days of filing the verified statement, the hospital must send a copy by registered mail to each person or entity alleged to be liable, the patient's attorney, and the Indiana Department of Insurance. Once these steps are completed, the hospital lien is perfected, giving the hospital the statutory right to recover its reasonable charges from any resulting settlement or judgment.

Additionally, Indiana Code § 32-33-4-3 provides an important protection for plaintiffs when hospital charges are so substantial that enforcing the lien would leave them with minimal compensation. Under this provision, if payment of the full hospital lien would result in the patient receiving less than 20% of the total settlement amount after deduction of attorney's fees and litigation expenses, the lien must be reduced to ensure that the patient retains at least 20% of the settlement proceeds. This safeguard preserves the fairness of the recovery process and prevents situations where an injured plaintiff walks away with virtually nothing after resolving a claim.

MEDICARE AND MEDICAID LIENS INTRODUCTION

If your client is covered by Medicare or Medicaid, these programs may initially pay for medical expenses related to their accident injuries. However, once your client's personal injury lawsuit or claim is resolved, Medicare or Medicaid may assert liens against the settlement proceeds to seek reimbursement for medical costs they previously paid on the client's behalf.

When Medicare or Medicaid is involved, you must notify the appropriate program that you represent the client and inquire whether any liens have been asserted. In many cases, these liens can be negotiated and reduced, which can significantly increase the client's net recovery.

In their book *Indiana Accident Law: A Reference for Accident Victims*, attorneys Paul Kruse and Tony Patterson of the law firm Parr Riche Obremskey Frandsen & Patterson LLP explain:

> If Medicare or Medicaid has paid health care providers for treatment you needed because of your accident, they are entitled to reimbursement of those payments from your claim. To ensure they are paid, they may assert a lien against your settlement. Your lawyer will need to hold back a portion of your settlement until you can negotiate an agreement with the lienholder.

MEDICARE LIENS

In personal injury cases involving a Medicare beneficiary, Medicare has a statutory right under the Medicare Secondary Payer (MSP) statute, 42 U.S.C. § 1395y(b), to recover conditional payments it made for accident-related medical care when another party was primarily responsible. Because this right is created by federal law, Medicare's lien—often referred to as a "super lien"—takes priority over other claims and is not subject to state lien-reduction statutes. Courts have consistently held that state laws do not limit Medicare's reimbursement rights. To initiate recovery, the Benefits Coordination & Recovery Center (BCRC) compiles a Conditional Payment Summary (CPS), which is a running total of the medical claims Medicare has paid that it believes are related to the injury. The CPS lists each payment by date of service, provider, diagnosis code, and amount paid, and is considered "conditional" because unrelated or duplicative charges can later be removed.

Medicare provides a secure online tool—the Medicare Secondary Payer Recovery Portal (MSPRP)—to help attorneys and beneficiaries efficiently manage these claims. Through the MSPRP, attorneys can report a case to the BCRC, view and download the CPS, dispute unrelated charges by uploading supporting documentation, and submit settlement information. This early review process is critical, as removing unrelated charges from the CPS can significantly reduce the lien amount. Once settlement documentation is submitted, Medicare issues a Final Demand Letter stating the precise amount to be reimbursed. Under 42 C.F.R. § 411.37, Medicare's recovery is reduced by a proportionate share of the procurement costs—attorney's fees and litigation expenses—incurred to obtain the settlement.

By carefully reviewing the CPS through the MSPRP, promptly disputing unrelated charges, and ensuring that procurement cost reductions are applied before paying the Final Demand, plaintiff's counsel can comply with Medicare's strict reimbursement rules while maximizing the client's net recovery.

MEDICAID LIENS IN PERSONAL INJURY CASES

In personal injury litigation, attorneys frequently encounter Medicaid liens. These statutory liens require reimbursement to state Medicaid programs for medical expenses paid on behalf of beneficiaries when those expenses arise from a third party's negligence. For example, the State of Indiana may assert a Medicaid lien against a portion of a client's settlement proceeds to recover amounts paid for the injury-related care. Below is an excerpt from a Medicaid lien letter in one of my personal injury cases, in which the State of Indiana asserted its right to reimbursement:

> Since our last follow up the Indiana Health Coverage Program (IHCP) has paid claims related to the incident. The subrogation amount is $177.19.

> Federal and state statutory and regulatory provisions allow the Indiana Family and Social Services Administration (FSSA) to assert and pursue a lien when a third party is legally responsible for payment of the medical expenses incurred by an IHCP member. The FSSA will pursue this case according to Ind. Code Sec. 12-15-8-1, et. seq., FSSA regulations 405 I.A.C. 1-1-1, 1-1-13, and 1-1-15, 42 USCA Sec. 1396a(A)(25), and 42 CFR Sec. 433.135.

In Indiana, Medicaid liens are governed primarily by Indiana Code Chapter 12-15-8, which establishes the state's right to place a lien on a beneficiary's recovery from a third party for medical expenses paid by Medicaid.

ERISA LIENS

The Employee Retirement Income Security Act of 1974 ("ERISA") is a federal law that governs various types of employee benefit plans, including retirement, health, life, and disability benefits. Many employers offer health insurance coverage through ERISA plans, which can significantly affect how settlements are distributed in personal injury cases.

When a client covered by an ERISA health plan is injured due to someone else's negligence and later receives a settlement, the ERISA plan may have a right to be reimbursed for the medical expenses it has already paid. This right is known as an ERISA lien.

In his insightful book, *How to Successfully Litigate a Personal Injury Case*, Attorney Andrew Smiley emphasizes the critical importance of identifying ERISA plans, stating, "There are certain types of private health insurance, ERISA plans in particular, that have a statutory right of a lien, so you need to find out if your client's health insurer is an ERISA plan. ERISA liens are very tough to negotiate down. I strongly recommend, if you have one of these liens, that you reach out to a lien resolution firm for guidance on how to handle the situation."

For lawyers, the first practical step is to always obtain a copy of your client's insurance benefit card. In addition, you should request a copy of the summary plan description or the plan document itself from the employer or plan administrator. The summary plan description is a document that ERISA requires employers to provide to plan participants. It explains in plain language how the plan works, what benefits it provides, and the rights and responsibilities of both the participant and the plan. The plan document, sometimes called the master plan or governing plan, is the actual legal document that outlines the specific terms, funding structure, and reimbursement rights. These documents will confirm whether the plan is governed by ERISA and whether it is insured or self-funded.

There are two main types of ERISA health plans: insured plans and self-funded plans. In an insured plan, the employer purchases a group insurance policy from a health insurance company. The employer and employees pay premiums to the insurer, and the insurer pays out medical claims. These plans are generally subject to state insurance laws and therefore subject to state statutory lien reduction laws.

In a self-funded plan, the employer pays medical claims directly using its own assets instead of buying insurance coverage. Self-funded ERISA plans are not subject to most state insurance laws. Because of this, self-funded plans often have stronger contractual rights to full reimbursement.

Understanding how these plans are structured is critical because it directly affects your client's net recovery. For instance, if your client's health coverage is provided through a self-funded ERISA plan, the employer may assert a lien for the full amount of medical expenses paid, recoverable directly from the settlement proceeds—potentially consuming the entire settlement. Self-funded ERISA plans are frequently adopted by large organizations, such as hospitals and banks, because they allow employers to better manage healthcare costs.

USING A LIEN REDUCTION LETTER

As a personal injury attorney, you may often need to negotiate medical liens on behalf of your clients. One common tool is a lien reduction letter, which allows you to request that the lienholder accept a reduced amount in full satisfaction of their claim.

Here's a basic structure you can use in your letter or email requesting a reduction from a lienholder:

It is my understanding that my client, [Client Name], has a lien with your company and that the outstanding balance is $[Current Lien Amount].

At this time, my client is offering $[Proposed Amount] to settle the outstanding balance as if it were paid in full.

If this is acceptable, please sign below and return this letter at your earliest convenience so that I can settle my client's claim and order the settlement check, after which we will pay your lien directly from our escrow account.

If the amount offered above is not acceptable, please indicate in the space at the end of this sentence the least acceptable amount: $_____.

After sending the letter by mail or email, you will typically receive a response from the lienholder. Most lienholders won't respond by filling out the letter directly, but they will often reply with their own written confirmation stating what amount they would accept as full settlement, and where to send the check. Sometimes they may request more information, such as a settlement breakdown or confirmation of the total settlement amount. While they rarely complete the letter as provided, sending a reduction request helps initiate the conversation and gets the ball rolling on reduction negotiations.

SUMMARY OF LISA SAMPSON'S CASE FOR MODULE 6

In Lisa Sampson's personal injury case, multiple liens required careful negotiation to ensure she retained the largest possible share of her settlement.

Lisa's health insurer, Anthem, initially asserted a $375 lien for accident-related medical expenses. Following negotiation, Anthem agreed to fully waive its lien, resulting in no reimbursement being required from Lisa's settlement proceeds. The Anthem lien was relatively small because Lisa's auto policy's Medical Payments (MedPay) coverage paid her medical bills up to its $5,000 limit, and Anthem likely benefited from contractual arrangements with medical providers that allowed it to pay significantly discounted rates.

Lisa's auto insurer, Erie Insurance, had issued payments under its MedPay coverage and asserted a $5,000 subrogation lien. However, upon our request, Erie Insurance agreed to waive its lien in full as an act of goodwill towards its insured, Lisa. This is an example of how strategically requesting a complete waiver of the lien, rather than merely a reduction, can be the most advantageous approach for maximizing the client's net recovery.

Chambers Medical Group, one of Lisa's treatment providers, originally charged $8,500 for its physical therapy services. After payments by Lisa's insurers, the outstanding lien balance was $2,500, which will be paid directly from the settlement proceeds.

Clark Memorial Hospital initially billed $2,500 for its services. After payments by insurance, an outstanding balance of $600 remained. However, because Clark Memorial Hospital did not perfect its claim under Indiana's Hospital Lien Statute, Lisa elected to pay this remaining balance directly, rather than through the law firm's settlement disbursement.

All other remaining balances with Yellow Ambulance, Radiology and Associates, Breg, Inc., Walgreens, and Strickland, Cox, and Associates were resolved in full through MedPay, health insurance payments, and provider write-offs.

As you can see, through diligent negotiation, our legal team secured strategic lien waivers and substantial reductions, significantly lowering Lisa's total obligations and maximizing her future net recovery from the settlement.

CONCLUSION OF MODULE 6

This concludes Module 6. In Module 7, we'll cover the process of filing the lawsuit.

THE LAWSUIT

INTRODUCTION TO FILING AND SERVING A PERSONAL INJURY LAWSUIT

Now we will discuss drafting, filing, and serving the lawsuit.

COMMON REASONS TO FILE A LAWSUIT

Why might you need to file a lawsuit? Some of the main reasons include preserving the statute of limitations, disagreements with the adjuster over your case's valuation, or disputes concerning the connection between the accident and your client's injuries—making it unlikely that the insurance company will offer a significant settlement without extensive discovery.

STATUTE OF LIMITATIONS

Under Indiana law, the statute of limitations for personal injury claims is two years from the date of the accident.

💡 PRACTICE TIP: Lawsuits Can Trigger a Change to the Adjuster

Here's another practice tip: if you're not having success obtaining the offer you want during pre-suit negotiations, filing a lawsuit will often result in a change in the adjuster handling the claim.

DRAFTING AND FILING THE COMPLAINT, APPEARANCE, AND SUMMONS

When filing a lawsuit, the initial documents required to begin the case include the complaint, the appearance of counsel, and the summons. The complaint is the formal legal document that begins the lawsuit. It sets forth the plaintiff's allegations, outlines the facts of the case, identifies the parties involved, and states the legal basis for holding the defendant liable. In a personal injury case, the plaintiff will file the complaint against the negligent driver who caused the collision. If the defendant was acting within the scope of their employment at the time of the accident, the employer should also be named as a defendant. Additionally, if your client has UM/UIM coverage, you will often want to include the client's auto insurer in the complaint when the value of the case justifies it.

Under Indiana Trial Rule 8(A), a complaint must include two basic elements: (1) a short and plain statement of the claim showing that the plaintiff is entitled to relief, and (2) a demand for the relief sought.

While some law firms use lengthy complaints, it is often preferable to keep the complaint brief so it can be easily tailored to the facts of each case.

Be sure to include a request for a jury trial at the end of your complaint. Also, make sure the case is filed in the proper venue—typically the county where the car accident occurred. For guidance on venue, consult Indiana Trial Rule 75.

To view the complaint filed to initiate litigation against Snake Jailbreak, please refer to Exhibit 7.

THE APPEARANCE

When initiating a personal injury lawsuit, plaintiff's counsel must e-file an appearance, which formally notifies the court – and opposing counsel upon their appearance – of who represents the plaintiff. Under Indiana Trial Rule 3.1, the appearance must include the name, address, telephone number, fax number, and email address of the party, as well as the same information for the attorney filing the appearance, including the attorney number. The form must also identify the case type, as classified by Administrative Rule 8(B)(3), and include a statement regarding whether the party will or will not accept service by fax or email. The appearance should also list all related cases with their captions and case numbers.

For a copy of the appearance entered on behalf of Lisa Sampson, see Exhibit 8.

THE SUMMONS

The procedures governing the issuance and service of a summons in a civil lawsuit are outlined in Indiana Trial Rules 4 through 4.17 and Rule 86. The most common method of serving a defendant is by sending the file-stamped complaint and summons via certified mail to the defendant's residence or place of employment. Two reliable ways to locate the defendant's current address is by using the crash report from the accident, as well as public search tools such as the one available by subscription on Westlaw.

If the lawsuit includes a claim against the defendant's employer, the employer's information can be obtained through the Indiana Secretary of State's online business entity search. This publicly accessible database lists all businesses registered in Indiana and provides both the principal office address and the registered agent's address on file. Under Indiana Trial Rule 4.6(A)(1), service on a business organization should be made on its registered agent. To view the summons served on Snake Jailbreak, please refer to Exhibit 9.

PROVING SERVICE BY CERTIFIED MAIL

After serving the defendant by certified mail, you will receive a signed return receipt (commonly referred to as the "green card") from the United States Postal Service. You should then electronically file the return receipt with the court as proof of service. This filing demonstrates that the defendant was properly served with the summons and complaint. The procedures governing service by certified mail are set forth in Indiana Trial Rule 4.11.

SERVING THROUGH THE SHERIFF

Occasionally, you'll need to serve the defendant through the sheriff. The process for this is outlined in Indiana Trial Rule 4.12.

SERVING BY PUBLICATION

If you are unable to serve the defendant by certified mail or through the sheriff, you may need to serve the defendant by publication. Indiana Trial Rule 4.13 governs this process. Service by publication is permitted in cases where the defendant cannot be found, has concealed their whereabouts, or has left the state, despite a diligent search.

The summons must be published three times in a newspaper authorized to publish legal notices in the county where the complaint is filed, where the defendant last resided, or where the property or issue in question is located. If no suitable newspaper is available in the relevant county, publication may occur in the nearest Indiana county with an appropriate publication or as directed by the court.

The return of service by publication must include affidavits from the newspaper confirming the dates and content of publication, as well as a statement that the publication met all legal requirements. These materials must be filed with the court and become part of the official record.

E-FILING THE LAWSUIT

To initiate a lawsuit in Indiana, you must prepare and file three key documents: the complaint, the appearance, and the summons. This can be done through Indiana's electronic filing system at efile.incourts.gov. Although other certified e-filing service providers are available, such as Doxpop, I generally use the state's e-filing portal.

Once you are on the e-filing website, log in or create an account, then follow the prompts to file your documents in the appropriate county. After your submission is reviewed and accepted by the county clerk, the clerk will sign the summons. You will receive an email notification containing a link to the signed summons.

After obtaining the signed summons, you must serve the defendant with both the file-stamped complaint and the signed summons. The most common method is to send these documents by certified mail to the defendant's residence or place of employment. When preparing the certified mailing, be sure to check both the "Certified Mail" and "Return Receipt for Merchandise" boxes on PS Form 3811 to ensure the post office returns the signed green card to your firm.

FILING PROOF OF SERVICE

After serving the defendant by certified mail, promptly e-file a notice of service with the court. The notice should state that service has been completed and include a copy of the green card (PS Form 3811) showing the defendant's signature.

In addition to the complaint and summons, include a brief cover letter in the same certified mail packet that you send to the defendant. This letter should explain to the defendant what the documents are and advise them of the next steps—such as notifying their insurance carrier or contacting your office if they are uninsured. As a professional courtesy, you should also provide a copy of the lawsuit to the liability insurance adjuster. This gives the adjuster an opportunity to respond quickly, whether by pursuing settlement or assigning defense counsel to appear in the case.

COMMON PERSONAL INJURY FILINGS

In a personal injury auto accident case, there are several common filings you can expect to encounter. Familiarizing yourself with these documents will help you better understand the procedural flow of litigation.

One of the first filings you might see from the defense is a Motion for Enlargement of Time, which asks the court for additional time to file a response to the complaint.

Next, you'll receive the defendant's Answer, which is their formal written response to your complaint. When reviewing the answer, pay close attention to whether defense counsel disputes the identity or legal capacity of the defendant. This is especially important in cases involving corporate defendants, who may operate under multiple names, subsidiaries, or related entities. Misidentifying the proper legal entity can be fatal to your case if the statute of limitations expires before the correct party is named in the Complaint.

One filing to familiarize yourself with is the Motion for Change of Judge. This is a formal request asking that the case be reassigned to a different judge, typically due to concerns about bias or a conflict of interest.

To advance the case, a party may file a Motion for Pretrial Conference, which asks the court to schedule a jury trial date. Setting a trial date helps keep the case moving forward and may motivate the defense to engage in settlement discussions.

In Marion County, Indiana, a Case Management Order must be filed. This order establishes deadlines for discovery, the filing of pretrial motions, and the disclosure of witnesses and exhibits. However, not every county in Indiana requires a case management order. Because procedures vary by jurisdiction, you should always review the local rules of the county where you are filing to determine whether a case management order is necessary.

As the case progresses, both sides will typically file Preliminary Witness and Exhibit Lists. These documents identify the individuals each party may call to testify and the evidence they may introduce at trial. The deadlines for these filings are usually set forth in the case management order.

Another common filing in personal injury cases is a Motion for Mediation, which asks the court to order the parties to participate in mediation in an effort to resolve the dispute before trial. Mediation is widely used in Indiana personal injury litigation and often leads to settlement. If the court orders mediation and the parties are unable to agree on a mediator, Indiana Alternative Dispute Resolution (ADR) Rule 2.4 provides that the court will designate a panel of three mediators. Each side then strikes one, and the remaining mediator is appointed. In practice, however, it is customary for counsel in Indiana personal injury cases to agree to mediation on their own, without the need to file a motion or involve the court.

FILING FOR DEFAULT JUDGMENT AND STRATEGIC CONSIDERATIONS

If the deadline for the defendant to answer the complaint passes without any response, the plaintiff may file for a default judgment under Indiana Trial Rule 55. A default judgment is a court order entered in favor of the plaintiff when the defendant fails to respond to the lawsuit. However, it is often advisable to delay filing for default judgment in a personal injury case. The reason is strategic: you generally want the defendant's insurance company to appear in the case so you can pursue a settlement with the liability insurer.

If a default judgment is entered before the insurer becomes involved, you may be left trying to collect directly from the defendant's personal assets, which is often impractical. Many defendants have little or no attachable assets, making them effectively "judgment-proof." Also be aware insurance policies often contain notice provisions or exclusions that may limit coverage if the insurer was not informed in a timely manner of the lawsuit by their insured. Most policies require the insured to promptly notify the insurer if a lawsuit has been filed. This notice is critical because it gives the insurer the opportunity to defend the case or settle before a judgment is entered. If the defendant fails to notify their insurer until after a default judgment is entered, the insurer will likely argue that it was prejudiced by the lack of notice and deny coverage.

For these reasons, the timing of a default judgment should be carefully considered. Waiting a reasonable period to allow the insurance company to appear may increase the likelihood of recovering damages through an insurance payout, rather than pursuing collection efforts directly against an individual defendant.

PRIORITY OF COVERAGE IN MULTI-POLICY AUTO ACCIDENTS

Situations often arise where two or more automobile insurance policies may provide coverage for the same incident. For example, if a vehicle owned by one person is being driven by another at the time of an accident, the vehicle owner's policy typically acts as the primary insurer, while the driver's policy serves as the secondary insurer.

As explained on StateFarm.com, "Typically, even if the person driving your car has their own insurance, your insurance will be the primary payer for damages caused by your vehicle. However, the person driving your car must be found legally at fault before your insurance will pay. The driver's insurance is secondary and may cover some personal injury or medical expenses. It may also provide coverage in excess of your insurance coverage if the cost of damages exceeds your policy limits."

To resolve conflicts when more than one policy applies to the same loss, most insurance policies contain an *"other insurance"* clause. This clause is designed to establish the order in which applicable insurance policies provide coverage.

Under Indiana Code § 27-8-9-7, the vehicle owner's insurance is considered primary if both of the following conditions are met: (1) the vehicle was operated with the owner's permission at the time the damage occurred, and (2) the use was within the scope of that permission. Additionally, Indiana Code § 27-8-9-9 governs insurance coverage priority for leased motor vehicles.

UM/UIM COVERAGE AND WAIVER

Now let's delve into uninsured and underinsured motorist (UM/UIM) coverage, which is a crucial component in many personal injury auto accident cases. In Indiana, insurance companies are required by law to offer UM/UIM coverage as part of any auto insurance policy. However, policyholders have the option to opt out of this coverage—but only if they do so in writing and in compliance with statutory requirements.

As a plaintiff's personal injury attorney, you should never assume that your client lacks UM/UIM coverage just because it isn't readily visible in the declarations page or summary of benefits. Unless your client explicitly waived this coverage in writing at the time the policy was issued or renewed—and in a form that complies with Indiana Code § 27-7-5-2—they may still be entitled to UM/UIM benefits.

UM coverage applies when the at-fault driver has no insurance, while UIM coverage comes into play when the at-fault driver's liability limits are insufficient to fully compensate your client for their injuries. If you determine that the at-fault driver is uninsured or underinsured, and your client has applicable UM/UIM coverage, you may need to assert a claim directly against your client's own auto insurance company.

FILING A UIM/UM COMPLAINT

When filing an uninsured or underinsured motorist claim against your client's auto insurance carrier, you should attach a copy of the insurance policy to the complaint if it is in the plaintiff's possession. This requirement arises from Indiana Trial Rule 9.2, which mandates that a written instrument forming the basis of a claim be included with the pleading or filed as an exhibit.

UNDERSTANDING HOW UM/UIM COVERAGE PAYS OUT

To understand how UM/UIM coverage is paid out to your client, consider the following illustration. Suppose the at-fault driver has $25,000 in liability coverage, and your client carries $100,000 in underinsured motorist coverage. In this scenario, your client may be eligible to claim up to $75,000 in additional benefits from their own insurer, assuming their damages exceed $25,000. However, don't get too excited—based on my experience, the plaintiff's own auto insurer often resists paying UM/UIM claims and will vigorously litigate to minimize its exposure. Note, underinsured motorist policies typically contain an exhaustion clause, requiring the at-fault driver's liability limits to be fully exhausted before UIM benefits become available.

PROTECTING THE UIM CARRIER'S SUBROGATION RIGHTS

A requirement under most auto insurance policies when UIM coverage is involved—is that the potential subrogation rights of the UIM carrier must be protected, or affirmatively waived by the carrier, before you can finalize a settlement with the at-fault party. This requirement stems from the principle that if the UIM carrier ultimately pays benefits to your client, it has the right to pursue reimbursement from the tortfeasor through subrogation. Therefore, it is incumbent upon you, as the attorney, to notify your client's UIM carrier of any offer to settle from the liability insurer. You must obtain the UIM carrier's consent before executing a release in favor of the tortfeasor. Releasing the tortfeasor without that consent can impair the carrier's subrogation rights and may ultimately bar your client from recovering UIM benefits.

Most UIM policies contain what's commonly referred to as a "consent-to-settle" or "notice-and-consent" provision. Once notified, the UIM carrier then has the option to either (1) waive its subrogation rights and allow the plaintiff to accept the third-party settlement and sign a release, or (2) "match" the third-party settlement offer by advancing that same amount to the plaintiff, while preserving the right to later pursue the tortfeasor to be fully reimbursed for the settlement money it had to pay out. In practice, this second option—where the UIM carrier advances the settlement funds—is rarely exercised, but the carrier must be given a meaningful opportunity to decide. Failing to provide this opportunity may result in a loss of UIM benefits for your client. By Indiana statute, the UIM carrier typically has 30 days to either consent to the settlement, allowing your client to accept the liability payment and pursue additional UM/UIM benefits if damages exceed the liability limit, or pay the settlement amount itself to preserve its subrogation rights.

To illustrate, imagine your client suffers $100,000 in damages, but the at-fault driver carries only $25,000 in liability coverage. Once the liability insurer tenders its $25,000 policy limits, you must notify your client's UIM carrier of that offer. At that point, the UIM carrier faces a choice. It can consent to the settlement, which allows your client to accept the $25,000 payment from the liability insurer and then pursue additional compensation under the UIM policy for the remaining damages. Alternatively, the UIM carrier may decide to "front" the $25,000 itself by paying it directly to your client. By doing so, the carrier preserves its right to pursue reimbursement from the at-fault driver. Suppose further that the UIM carrier determines your client is entitled to an additional $10,000 in UIM benefits. In that scenario, the carrier would pay your client a total of $35,000—consisting of the $25,000 liability amount it advanced plus the $10,000 in UIM coverage. Having stepped into your client's shoes for the $25,000 liability payment, the UIM carrier may then bring an action against the at-fault driver to recover the full $35,000. This process ensures your client receives timely compensation without sacrificing the carrier's ability to protect its subrogation rights against the negligent driver.

To learn more about this procedure, see Indiana Code § 27-7-5-6.

SECOND SETTLEMENT OFFER IN LISA SAMPSON CASE

We have some positive news regarding Lisa's case. After filing the lawsuit on January 19, 2025, we received a new settlement offer of $22,000 in May 2025. During the period between January and May, Unique Insurance requested that our firm refrain from litigating further until the adjuster could provide an updated settlement figure, to which our firm agreed.

We had hoped that Unique Insurance would offer the full $25,000 policy limits; however, instead of tendering the full amount, they chose to test whether we would compromise on our position. Based on this new offer, and after accounting for liens, case expenses, and a reduction in the attorney fee to ensure that our firm does not recover more than the client, Lisa would have received approximately one-third of the settlement proceeds.

After discussing the offer with Lisa and explaining that we believe she can receive the full policy limits, she decided to reject the offer and proceed with further litigation.

☀ PRACTICE TIP: Responding to an Inadequate Settlement Offer

Here's another practice tip you can use: If you find that the defense's offer is unworkable, consider sending a detailed breakdown to defense counsel—and, with permission, to the adjuster—explaining why the offer is insufficient. This breakdown should clearly demonstrate how and why the offer fails to meet your client's needs. By highlighting the shortfall, you make it evident that the offer must be increased for your client to seriously consider settlement.

SUMMARY OF LISA SAMPSON'S CASE FOR MODULE 7

In Module 7, Lisa Sampson's personal injury case progressed from pre-suit negotiations into formal litigation. After sending a demand letter and receiving an initial settlement offer of $14,300, we filed a lawsuit on January 19, 2025, to preserve the statute of limitations and apply pressure against Unique insurance for a better resolution.

After filing the complaint, appearance, and summons through the Indiana E-Filing System, our firm served the defendant, Snake Jailbreak, with the lawsuit by certified mail. This prompted renewed settlement discussions with Unique Insurance. At the liability insurer's request, our firm agreed to pause further action in the lawsuit while the liability adjuster calculated a new settlement figure. Ultimately, Unique Insurance extended a new offer of $22,000. However, after discussing this offer with Lisa and advising her of her right to pursue the full $25,000 policy limits, she chose to reject the offer and continue litigating her claim.

END OF MODULE 7

This concludes Module 7. In Module 8, we will begin our discussion on discovery.

DISCOVERY

INTRODUCTION TO MODULE 8

In Module 8, we will focus on discovery. Indiana Trial Rule 26 outlines the various discovery methods available and defines the scope of discovery. Generally, any information relevant to the case is subject to discovery, even if it may not be admissible in court.

INTERROGATORIES AND REQUEST FOR PRODUCTION OF DOCUMENTS

Interrogatories and requests for production of documents are typically served on defense counsel shortly after the lawsuit is filed. In turn, defense counsel will usually serve a corresponding set of discovery requests on the plaintiff.

Plaintiff attorneys should keep in mind that defense counsel often provide responses to interrogatories and requests for production that are limited in substance. As Steven Burris observed in *Automobile Accident Cases in Las Vegas*, "Requests for Production of Documents oftentimes are as useless as interrogatories in today's world." From my experience, the documentation produced by defense counsel in response to discovery requests is usually minimal. Typically, you may receive the crash report, a few photographs, and repair estimates for the defendant's vehicle.

With respect to what plaintiff's counsel should provide to defense counsel when responding to their discovery request, I think it's best practice to produce almost everything you have in your file. I remember one time a plaintiff's personal injury attorney telling me at mediation that he doesn't try to hide the ball and finds it easier to be thorough in what he produces in discovery. This sentiment has also been expressed by top lawyers in the industry as well. Attorney Justin Ziegler, one of Florida's top personal injury attorneys, operates a YouTube channel with hundreds of videos offering advice on how to handle personal injury claims. In one of his videos, Ziegler emphasized the importance of providing liability insurance companies with all the necessary information to properly document their files.

Top trucking accident attorney Joseph Fried has expressed a similar view in his lectures. Fried advised attorneys to send the adjuster everything they have—making it easy for the adjuster to locate photos, medical bills, and, if a lawsuit has been filed, deposition testimony—in order to educate the adjuster about the case.

🔆 PRACTICE TIP: Interrogatory Questions

Attorneys often wonder how many interrogatory questions they are allowed to serve. The Indiana Trial Rules do not specify a limit on the number of interrogatories. However, some counties have local rules that impose limits. For example, in Allen County, Indiana, the maximum number of interrogatory questions—including subparts—is 50.

In federal court, the limit is 25 interrogatory questions, including subparts, as set forth in Rule 33 of the Federal Rules of Civil Procedure.

INTERROGATORY INSIGHTS

In his book *Automobile Accident Cases in Las Vegas*, Attorney Steven Burris observed that serving interrogatories on defense counsel has become largely ineffective, as defense attorneys have become highly skilled at crafting non-substantive responses. However, Georgia personal injury attorney Mike Rafi offers a useful counterpoint. Through his YouTube channel, which features a wide range of instructional videos on personal injury practice, Rafi shared practical insights on how to make interrogatories more effective. In one video specifically focused on interrogatory strategy, he explains that he limits his questions to a concise list, each aimed at obtaining specific and meaningful information. He avoids overly broad or generic questions, preferring instead to reserve those topics for depositions.

Rafi also notes that in many of his cases, he begins scheduling depositions immediately after filing the complaint, often before issuing any written discovery.

He also emphasizes that he rarely objects to discovery questions when answering them from defense counsel—except where attorney-client privilege applies.

It is worth noting, however, that Rafi typically handles high-value cases, where the cost of early depositions is justified by the potential recovery. In smaller cases, where litigation budgets are tighter, initiating discovery with written requests may remain the more practical approach.

With interrogatory responses from defense counsel, you may frequently encounter objections such as: "Defendant objects to this interrogatory because it calls for the defendant to make a legal conclusion." However, Indiana Trial Rule 33(D) explicitly states that "an interrogatory otherwise proper is not objectionable merely because an answer to the interrogatory involves an opinion, contention, or legal conclusion." Therefore, objections based solely on the assertion that a question calls for a legal conclusion are rarely valid.

If defense counsel raises this objection and you still want a response, you can cite Indiana Trial Rule 33(D) to challenge it. Additionally, be mindful of Indiana Trial Rule 26(E), which requires counsel to supplement their discovery responses under certain circumstances. Explaining Trial Rules 33 and 26 to opposing counsel—especially when they fail to disclose sufficient information—can help apply pressure on the defense to take the responses seriously and may even encourage earlier settlement.

OBJECTING TO INTERROGATORIES AND REQUESTS FOR PRODUCTION OF DOCUMENTS

In responding to written discovery, plaintiff's counsel may need to assert objections based on privileged information. Two of the most common privileges invoked are the attorney-client privilege and the attorney work product doctrine. These doctrines protect confidential legal communications and materials prepared in anticipation of litigation.

An objection based on attorney-client privilege might read: "The plaintiff objects to this interrogatory on the grounds that it seeks information protected by the attorney-client privilege. The interrogatory calls for confidential communications made for the purpose of obtaining legal advice, which are not subject to disclosure."

For the work product doctrine, an appropriate objection could state: "The plaintiff objects to this request to the extent it seeks attorney work product prepared in anticipation of litigation or for trial. The defendant has not demonstrated a substantial need for this information or shown that it cannot obtain the substantial equivalent by other means without undue hardship."

Counsel should always evaluate whether the objection is warranted under the facts and circumstances of the case. Where possible, non-privileged and responsive information should be produced.

OBTAINING CELL PHONE RECORDS

There are two primary methods for obtaining cell phone usage data in motor vehicle accident cases. The first involves obtaining the device along with its password and having a forensic company copy its contents. This process can reveal whether the phone was in use at the time of the collision, including whether the defendant driver was texting, browsing the internet, or watching a video, among other activities. *Understanding Motor Carrier Claims* (7th ed.), authored by Joseph Fried and Michael L. Goldberg, contains an excellent chapter on this process entitled "Cellphone

Evidence." The second–and more common method for car accident cases–
is to subpoena the defendant driver's cell phone carrier. Although written
discovery to the defendant may include requests for cell phone records,
defense counsel rarely produces them in discovery responses. To obtain
this critical information, you will need to issue a subpoena directly to
the carrier. The defendant's service provider can be identified through
interrogatories or during the defendant's deposition. Records obtained
from the carrier should include details of calls and text messages sent or
received, as well as cell tower data indicating the device's location at the
time each call or text occurred.

MOTIONS TO COMPEL

In the course of personal injury litigation, it is common for defense
counsel to provide incomplete, evasive, or untimely responses to discovery
requests. When informal efforts to resolve these issues fail, the next step
for plaintiff's counsel is to file a motion to compel.

Before filing such a motion in Indiana state court, Indiana Trial Rule
26(F) requires the moving party to first make a reasonable effort to reach
agreement with the opposing party concerning the matter. The purpose
of this requirement is to demonstrate that counsel has made a good-faith
effort to resolve the dispute without court intervention. More broadly,
Trial Rule 26 sets out the general framework for discovery in Indiana,
including the methods of discovery available, the scope of information that
may be obtained, protections for privileged and work product material,
discovery concerning experts, procedures for protective orders, and the
duty to supplement responses.

A properly drafted motion to compel should clearly outline the
discovery requests at issue, describe the deficiencies in the responses,
and explain the relevance of the information sought.

In practice, the simple act of filing a motion to compel often prompts
defense counsel to produce the requested documentation, rendering a
court hearing unnecessary. As a result, motions to compel can be an

effective tool for applying pressure and moving the case forward when discovery has stalled.

⚡ PRACTICE TIP: Attempting Discovery Resolution

Judges generally expect attorneys to make a genuine effort to resolve discovery disputes informally. Repeated or premature filings without attempting resolution can reflect poorly on counsel and may even result in sanctions or denial of the motion.

For further guidance on compelling discovery, see Indiana Trial Rule 37, which governs motions to compel and authorizes sanctions for failing to comply with discovery obligations.

NARRATIVE REPORT

During the discovery phase of litigation, providing a physician's narrative report to the opposing party can be a highly effective strategy. A narrative report is a critical document frequently submitted to the at-fault party's insurance company during settlement negotiations, and it can serve as a powerful tool in advocating for a fair resolution of your client's claim.

The report should clearly establish a causal connection between the car accident and the client's injuries. It must also address the reasonableness and necessity of the medical treatment provided, as well as outline any anticipated future care. If applicable, the physician should assign a permanent impairment rating, which can significantly impact the overall valuation of the claim.

When your client requires ongoing treatment, it is essential that the narrative includes detailed estimates of future medical expenses. This helps emphasize the long-term financial impact of the injuries and strengthens your position during settlement discussions.

A well-prepared and thoroughly documented physician's narrative report can carry substantial weight with insurance adjusters and may serve as the foundation for maximizing your client's recovery.

INDEPENDENT MEDICAL EXAM (IME)

In personal injury cases, it is common during the discovery phase for the defense to request an independent medical examination (IME). An IME is a medical evaluation performed by a physician who has not been involved in the patient's care. Its purpose is to provide an opinion on the nature and extent of the patient's injuries, the reasonableness of the treatment received, the expected date of maximum medical improvement, the likelihood of full or partial recovery, and the degree of any permanent impairment.

Under Rule 35 of the Indiana Rules of Trial Procedure, a defendant has the right to request an IME and select the examining physician. However, this process is not without criticism. Attorney Evan Aidman, in *Winning Personal Injury Cases*, argues that these examinations should be described as Defense Medical Exams, given that the physicians are often selected and paid by insurance companies. Aidman contends that these doctors are frequently "hired guns" who are motivated to deliver findings that align with the insurer's interests.

Although IMEs are usually initiated by the defense, plaintiff's counsel may also arrange for an exam by an independent physician who has not previously treated the client. This is often done to provide an expert medical opinion to the opposing side or to rebut a biased IME.

NOTICE OF DEPOSITION

In *Winning Personal Injury Cases*, attorney Evan Aidman emphasizes that depositions are the most important component of discovery. He highlights the value of deposing the defendant to uncover the insurance company's version of the accident and to better assess the strengths and weaknesses of the case. Similarly, Steven Burris, in *Automobile Accident Cases in Las Vegas*, underscores that the primary purpose of a deposition by plaintiff's counsel is "to lock in the other side's story" and to establish "the main points you want to make about your own case."

To schedule the defendant's deposition, begin by coordinating a mutually agreeable date with defense counsel. Once a date is set, contact a court reporter service to arrange coverage of the deposition. It is advisable to request that the deposition be videotaped, as video testimony can be especially powerful if used at trial or in settlement discussions. After confirming arrangements with the court reporter, prepare and serve the notice of deposition on defense counsel.

Depositions by oral examination are governed by Indiana Trial Rule 30, which permits parties to depose any person with knowledge relevant to the litigation—including both parties and non-parties. This rule outlines procedures for questioning, recording and objecting during the deposition process. Rule 30 should be read in conjunction with Indiana Trial Rule 32, which addresses the permissible uses of depositions in later proceedings, such as at trial or in hearings of a motion.

DEPOSITION TIPS

One quote I want to highlight from *The Complete Personal Injury Practice Manual* by Al J. Cone and Verne Lawyer states, "In taking the adverse party's deposition, the attorney should plan the questions in advance, in logical sequence, categorizing them according to the information desired." Many attorneys fail to do this and instead walk into a deposition without a prepared list of questions. However, in all of my depositions, I draft my questions beforehand and prepare exhibits for use during the examination.

Another helpful tip from *The Complete Personal Injury Practice Manual* states: "If a damaging admission is obtained from the witness, and the attorney is certain that the witness has fully understood the question, the attorney should drop the subject immediately and go on to something else. The witness can explain why he gave the answer he did at the time of trial." This approach prevents the defendant from mitigating the harmful admission by offering clarifications in response to follow-up questions.

In his book *How to Successfully Litigate a Personal Injury Case*, attorney Andrew Smiley offers practical and insightful guidance on preparing for and conducting depositions as well. Smiley underscores the critical importance of thoroughly preparing your client before the deposition. He recommends spending at least one hour in preparation, during which the client should reflect on how the injuries have impacted their daily life. Clients should be encouraged to describe their injuries in practical terms and offer specific examples—such as difficulty walking, lifting, or sleeping—to illustrate how their physical limitations interfere with everyday functioning.

He also stresses the importance of teaching clients how to testify effectively. This includes keeping answers brief and on point, avoiding speculation, and maintaining a polite and respectful demeanor throughout the deposition. Preparing your client to address potential weaknesses in their case is equally essential. Smiley advises candid discussions about any problematic facts so that the client is ready to present those issues in the most favorable and truthful light.

When it comes to conducting the deposition of the defendant, Smiley recommends organizing all exhibits in advance and working from a structured outline of questions. This ensures a logical flow and comprehensive coverage of all relevant topics. Templates and sample outlines for deposing a defendant driver are readily available online and can serve as a helpful starting point for structuring your examination.

Smiley also notes that it is extremely rare for a defendant to admit fault during a deposition. Therefore, the goal is not to elicit confessions, but rather to lock in testimony, uncover the defense's version of events, and expose inconsistencies. Smiley rarely objects to questions posed by opposing counsel during his client's deposition, finding that uninterrupted questioning often leads to a more efficient and productive session.

Ultimately, a well-prepared deposition can yield critical information, clarify contested facts, and provide insights that significantly influence case strategy and settlement value.

THE NECESSITY OF EXPERT TESTIMONY IN INDIANA PERSONAL INJURY LITIGATION

If you're taking a personal injury auto accident case to trial in Indiana, you will almost always want to present expert medical testimony regarding your client's injuries. While not strictly required in every case, medical expert testimony is often critical—particularly when it comes to establishing causation.

Under Indiana law, whether medical expert testimony is legally required depends on the nature of the injury: whether it is objective or subjective.

A subjective injury is one experienced by the patient but not directly observable by the physician, such as chronic pain, headaches, or emotional distress. These types of injuries cannot be verified through a physical examination alone and typically rely on the plaintiff's own description of symptoms. In such cases, lay testimony alone is not sufficient to establish a causal connection between the accident and the injury. Indiana courts typically require expert medical testimony to establish causation for subjective injuries, such as pain, emotional distress, or soft tissue injuries, which lack objective verification. Without expert testimony linking the injury to the accident, the plaintiff's case may not survive summary judgment or a motion for directed verdict, particularly where the injury is not clearly within the understanding of a lay jury.

An objective injury, by contrast, is one that can be discovered through a physical examination, independent of the patient's self-reporting—for example, a broken bone or a visible laceration. In these situations, the plaintiff is competent to testify about the injury, and lay testimony may be sufficient for the jury to reach a verdict without expert medical evidence.

Even in cases involving objective injuries, it is advisable to introduce medical expert testimony. Jurors may expect to hear from a doctor to validate the severity and ongoing impact of the injuries. Expert testimony also adds credibility and clarity to your case, helping the jury understand the medical issues involved and reinforcing your client's claims.

An experienced medical expert can testify not only to causation but also to the necessity of treatment, future medical needs, permanent impairment, and prognosis—all of which are relevant to damages.

In Indiana, whether expert medical testimony is required depends on the objectivity of the injury, but as a practical matter, it is almost always beneficial. To maximize your chances of success at trial—and to withstand motions challenging your evidence on causation—it is best practice to retain a qualified medical expert to support your client's claims.

LINKING THE INJURY TO THE ACCIDENT

Even when a plaintiff presents medical expert testimony at trial, a personal injury case can still fail if causation is not adequately established. It is not enough to simply have a doctor testify; the testimony must satisfy Indiana's legal standards for proving a causal link between the accident and the alleged injuries.

The Indiana Court of Appeals decision in *Topp v. Leffers*, 838 N.E.2d 1027 (Ind. Ct. App. 2005), illustrates this principle. In that case, the plaintiff, Yvonne Topp, claimed injuries resulting from a motor vehicle collision. However, her injuries were subjective in nature—meaning they could not be directly observed through physical examination. Under Indiana law, subjective injuries require expert medical testimony to establish causation; a plaintiff's lay testimony alone is insufficient.

In that case, Ms. Topp had a history of pre-existing injuries, making causation a complex medical issue beyond the understanding of a lay juror. Due to this complexity, the court required expert testimony specifically addressing whether the accident caused or aggravated her injuries to a reasonable degree of medical certainty.

Although Ms. Topp did present expert testimony from a physician who conducted an independent medical examination and from her primary care physician, their testimony fell short of the required standard. The physicians stated only that her injuries "apparently," "appeared," "possibly," or "may" have been aggravated by the accident. The court held that such speculative language was insufficient to prove causation. Indiana law requires that expert testimony establish causation with reasonable medical certainty or probability; evidence based merely on possibility or speculation cannot support a verdict. This case serves as an important reminder that the quality and clarity of expert testimony matter as much as its mere existence. Vague or noncommittal opinions—even when offered by qualified physicians—will not satisfy the plaintiff's burden of proof.

In personal injury litigation, establishing a causal connection between your client's injuries and the accident is essential to securing a favorable verdict. This step often hinges on the strength and clarity of your medical expert's testimony. To meet the plaintiff's burden of proof, your medical expert must testify that, to a reasonable degree of medical certainty, the injuries resulted from the accident. Anything less—such as terms like "possible" or "probable"—is not sufficient if offered in isolation.

In *Palace Bar, Inc. v. Fearnot*, 381 N.E.2d 858 (Ind. 1978), the Indiana Supreme Court emphasized that a doctor's conclusion can be considered evidence only when it is based on a reasonable medical certainty that a fact is true or untrue.

The reasoning behind this rule is clear: causation is often a technical and complex issue, not within the ordinary understanding of lay jurors. As articulated in *Daub v. Daub*, 629 N.E.2d 873 (Ind. Ct. App. 1994), expert medical testimony is required when the causal connection between an injury and the tort is not obvious or within the jury's life experience.

While expert opinions using terms like "possible" or "probable" are not sufficient on their own, they may contribute to a finding of causation if combined with other competent evidence. For example, when a plaintiff testifies credibly about how their symptoms began immediately after the accident, and the medical expert supports that account as consistent with the type of trauma sustained, the cumulative evidence may meet the legal threshold.

The following excerpts from a deposition illustrate how plaintiff's counsel can use precise legal and medical terminology—such as "reasonable medical certainty" and "reasonable, medically necessary, and directly related"–to ensure that a medical expert properly connects the plaintiff's injuries and treatment to the automobile accident.

These terms are not merely formalities. Under Indiana law, they are essential to meeting the evidentiary burden on issues of causation and damages. Proper phrasing helps ensure the testimony is both admissible and persuasive.

The exchange below comes from an actual deposition taken in an Indiana auto accident case:

> Plaintiff's Attorney: Doctor, based on your education, training, and experience, do you believe, to a reasonable degree of medical certainty, that Mr. Tyler's complaints of lumbar pain, which began on or shortly after April 3, 2006, are causally related to the automobile collision involving Mr. Byrd?
>
> Medical Expert: Yes.
>
> Plaintiff's Attorney: With respect to the records marked as Plaintiff's Exhibit No. 1, in your professional opinion, was the treatment documented in those records reasonable, medically necessary, and directly related to the April 3, 2006 automobile accident?
>
> Medical Expert: Yes.

This line of questioning establishes causation with the required standard of "reasonable medical certainty," connects the plaintiff's treatment to the collision, and affirms that the care provided was both reasonable and necessary.

PRACTICE TIP: Building a Strong Doctor List for Personal Injury Litigation

On the subject of choosing treating physicians, Attorney Evan Aidman advises:

> "After an accident, it is desirable if your clients choose their doctors themselves. This helps avoid the appearance that the medical care was undertaken merely to build a legal case. Often, though, clients will want you to make a referral. Do not hesitate to do so. You must begin building a list of reputable doctors who will cooperate in litigation."

For example, at Isaacs & Isaacs, one of the firm's trial attorneys regularly scheduled independent medical examinations (IMEs) for clients with a physician affiliated with the University of Louisville. Developing relationships with reputable and cooperative physicians can be an important part of building solid medical foundations for your cases.

STRATEGIC PREPARATION OF TREATING PHYSICIANS FOR DEPOSITIONS

Before deposing your medical expert, attorney Scott Starr advises that plaintiff's counsel should meet with each of the plaintiff's primary treating physicians. As Starr explains in *Common Mistakes Plaintiff's Lawyers Sometimes Make* (ICLEF: *The Automobile Injury Case)*, "Plaintiff's counsel should spend some time with each of plaintiff's chief treating doctors to candidly discuss the strengths and weaknesses of plaintiff's medical case." This preparation not only ensures that the attorney understands the medical nuances but also allows for strategic planning regarding the presentation of medical evidence. A well-prepared treating physician can serve as a powerful anchor for your client's injury claims. Starr further recommends that when a treating physician proves to be a particularly strong witness for the plaintiff, counsel should schedule the doctor's deposition before mediation. Doing so allows the defendant—and more importantly, the insurance adjuster—to incorporate the favorable testimony into their valuation of the claim. By locking in persuasive expert testimony in advance, plaintiff's counsel may increase the likelihood of achieving a favorable settlement.

It's also worth remembering that juries tend to give more weight to the testimony of a primary care or treating physician than to that of a physician retained solely for litigation purposes. This principle is widely recognized in the legal community. As noted in *The Complete Personal Injury Practice Manual*, testimony from a treating physician is typically regarded as more credible than that of a physician who examined the plaintiff only for the purpose of providing expert testimony. For this reason, investing time and care into selecting and preparing treating physicians can significantly enhance the persuasive power of your client's case to the insurer.

REQUEST FOR ADMISSIONS

Let's now turn our attention to requests for admissions, an often underutilized discovery tool that can streamline trial preparation and reduce evidentiary hurdles.

In his book *Winning Personal Injury Cases*, attorney Evan Aidman illustrates the strategic value of requests for admissions in clarifying undisputed facts and simplifying the presentation of evidence. He writes:

> "Requests for admissions can be very productive discovery devices. They are used to get the other side to admit or deny specific facts, opinions or the application of law to fact. They help to clarify matters that are not in dispute and, thus, avoid unnecessary proof at trial. For example, all evidence must be authenticated before it can be admitted for the jury's consideration. If you wish to offer a photograph into evidence, you must first prove that it is an authentic rendition of what you suggest it depicts. This may require that the person who took the photo testify about the events surrounding the taking of the photo. If the other side admits that the photo is authentic, you do not need to bring this person to court to testify. That saves time and money, which both the judge and jury will appreciate."

Aidman's example highlights the utility of requests for admissions in eliminating the need to call live witnesses for foundational matters—especially when those matters are not truly in dispute.

In personal injury litigation, requests for admissions can be particularly effective in laying the groundwork to admit medical bills into evidence without unnecessary objections or authentication issues. For instance, a plaintiff may serve the defendant with a complete set of medical bills related to the injuries claimed and then request that the defendant admit: that the bills are authentic, that the medical services were necessary, and that the charges are reasonable.

As a practical resource, *The Complete Personal Injury Practice Manual* by Al Cone and Verne Lawyer includes a sample request for admissions specifically tailored to authenticate medical records for trial.

DEFENDANT'S NONPARTY REQUEST FOR PRODUCTION AND SUBPOENA DUCES TECUM

As plaintiff's counsel in Indiana personal injury cases, you will often receive requests from defense counsel seeking access to your client's medical, employment, or other records from nonparties. These requests are governed by the Indiana Rules of Trial Procedure, specifically Trial Rule 34(C) and Trial Rule 45(B). Together, these rules establish a process for obtaining documents from nonparties, and it is important for plaintiff's counsel to understand how the procedures work in tandem to protect the client's privacy interests while ensuring compliance with discovery rules.

Trial Rule 34(C) authorizes a party to request production of documents from a nonparty, such as a medical provider. However, this rule also contains procedural safeguards. Before serving the nonparty, the requesting party must serve plaintiff's counsel with a copy of the proposed request and subpoena at least fifteen days in advance. This notice requirement gives plaintiff's counsel time to review the request and object if necessary. If no objection is made within that period, the requesting party may proceed with service on the nonparty. In practice, it is common for plaintiff's counsel to waive the fifteen-day notice period by email if the request is routine and noncontroversial, thereby allowing defense counsel to move forward without delay. In addition, Rule 34(C)(4) requires that once documents are produced by a nonparty, the receiving party must provide copies to all other parties named in the lawsuit within fifteen days.

While Rule 34(C) sets out the procedural requirements, a request by itself does not compel a nonparty to produce records. This is where Trial Rule 45(B) comes into play. A subpoena duces tecum, which literally means "bring with you under penalty," is a court-issued order that legally requires a nonparty to produce the requested documents or tangible things. Rule 45(B) also gives the court discretion to quash or modify a subpoena if it is unreasonable or oppressive. Thus, Rule 34(C) ensures proper notice and fairness, while Rule 45(B) provides the enforcement mechanism to compel compliance.

🔆 PRACTICE TIP: Laying a Foundation

Many attorneys fear not being able to get evidence admitted, but the standard for laying a foundation is relatively straightforward. Under Indiana Rule of Evidence 901(a), the proponent of the evidence must establish only a reasonable probability that the evidence is what it is claimed to be. This can be shown through direct or circumstantial evidence. As stated in *Richardson v. State*, 79 N.E.3d 958 (Ind. Ct. App. 2017), absolute proof of authenticity is not required. Instead, the offering party need only demonstrate a reasonable likelihood that the document or item is what it purports to be.

🔆 PRACTICE TIP: Introducing an Exhibit

Introducing an exhibit at trial requires following a clear and orderly process to ensure the court has an adequate foundation for admitting the evidence. The first step is to describe the exhibit for the record. For example, you might begin by stating, "Your Honor, I'm holding a photograph showing the intersection where the cars collided." Once the item is identified, you should ask the court's permission to have it marked for identification, such as by saying, "Your Honor, may I approach the clerk and have the photograph marked as Plaintiff's Exhibit 1?"

After the exhibit is marked, you must show it to opposing counsel before presenting it to the witness. A common way to do this is by stating, "Your Honor, may the record reflect that I am showing the exhibit to opposing counsel?" Once that step is completed, you'll then ask permission to approach the witness, typically saying, "Your Honor, may I approach the witness?"

With permission granted, you hand the exhibit to the witness and begin laying the foundation through testimony. Foundational questions for a photograph may include: "Mrs. White, I'm showing you Plaintiff's Exhibit 1. Do you recognize the scene in this photograph?" Follow up with, "What scene does it show?" and then, "Does the photo fairly and accurately show how that intersection looked at the time of the collision?" If the witness confirms that the photograph is accurate and depicts the scene as it appeared at the relevant time, the foundation is established.

The final step is to offer the exhibit into evidence. You do this by stating, "Your Honor, we offer Plaintiff's Exhibit 1 into evidence." At that point, opposing counsel may object, or the court may admit the exhibit without objection.

SUMMARY OF LISA SAMPSON'S CASE FOR MODULE 8

In Module 8, Lisa Sampson's case advanced into the discovery phase. After the complaint was filed, Unique Insurance contacted our firm requesting a temporary pause in litigation while it prepared a new settlement offer. We agreed to the brief hold; however, the insurer's revised offer did not reflect policy limits, and with Lisa's consent, we promptly declined.

Following our rejection of the second offer, our team immediately served interrogatories and requests for production of documents on defense counsel. As is common in many personal injury cases, the responses we received back were limited in substance. Around the same time, Lisa was required to respond to the defense's written discovery requests. Unlike many defense attorneys retained by liability insurers, our plaintiff's firm takes pride in providing comprehensive, good-faith responses to interrogatories and requests for production of documents. For example, in our response to the defense's requests for production, we produced extensive documentation, downloading nearly the entire case file onto a flash drive and delivering it to opposing counsel. This flash drive included photographs of Lisa and her vehicle, complete lien ledgers, all medical bills and records, the entire original demand packet with all exhibits, intake documentation, and other miscellaneous documentation in the file.

This robust level of disclosure aligns with best practices taught by some of America's most accomplished personal injury attorneys. Sharing virtually the entire case file demonstrates credibility and readiness, and it can strengthen the plaintiff's position by highlighting the thoroughness of our case preparation.

After both sides exchanged and answered interrogatories and document requests, defense counsel requested that Lisa appear for a deposition. In response, our firm scheduled the deposition of the defendant Snake Jailbreak. Defense counsel then coordinated with us to set mutually convenient dates for the depositions and we both issued formal Notices of Deposition. Both depositions were scheduled for October 2025 but ultimately did not take place because the case settled beforehand. Neither party served requests for admissions during discovery.

Overall, the discovery process in Lisa's case was managed strategically to secure key evidence, reinforce the strength of her claims, and preserve negotiating leverage. These diligent efforts laid the groundwork for the final resolution of her claim.

END OF MODULE 8

This concludes Module 8. In Module 9, we will discuss mediation and the settlement of a personal injury claim.

MEDIATION AND SETTLEMENT

INTRODUCTION TO MEDIATION AND SETTLEMENT

Now that we have addressed the key aspects of discovery, Module 9 will explore mediation and settlement.

SHOULD YOU MEDIATE?

Just because you schedule a mediation doesn't mean the adjuster will show up and make a reasonable offer. Mediation can be expensive—especially in cases with thin margins—so it is often better to simply pick up the phone and try to work out the settlement without involving a mediator.

A top personal injury trial attorney from Kentucky went so far as to say that he won't even agree to mediation unless the other side first commits to putting a good-faith offer on the table. He explained that when he was starting out as a personal injury lawyer, he always agreed to mediation, believing that everyone came with the intention of reaching a fair resolution. However, as he gained experience, he realized that many mediations were becoming a waste of time.

If you decide to attend mediation, my main advice is to make sure you go in with the final numbers on your client's medical bills and liens. Having these figures readily available allows you to quickly calculate how much your client will receive in their pocket based on any settlement offer. Occasionally, though, the outstanding lien amount may be so substantial that the lienholder refuses to offer a reduction before mediation, instead electing to wait until they know the actual settlement figure. In that situation, you should notify the lienholder of the mediation date and provide the mediator with the lienholder's contact information so the mediator can call during the session to try to reach a final lien amount. A good mediator will offer this service. My two favorite mediators, Larry Church and Paul Petticrew, both were exceptionally skilled at negotiating with lienholders to reduce liens and facilitate case resolution.

Before the mediation, you should provide the mediator and defense counsel with a summary of all liens and outstanding medical bills. In addition, you should send another demand letter to defense counsel and the adjuster at least a month before the mediation date to give them time to evaluate the claim and place a proper reserve on it.

One critical point to remember when preparing for mediation is to request the adjuster's presence at the session. Doing so will likely prompt the adjuster to thoroughly review your case in advance and come prepared with settlement authority.

At mediation, you generally do not need to make an opening statement, as it is unlikely anything said will affect the outcome. The only exception is when you have an unreasonable client. In that scenario, it may be helpful for them to hear defense counsel point out the weaknesses in the case, which can help temper expectations and provide a more realistic sense of their cases value.

KEYS TO MEDIATION: FINAL MEDICAL BILLS AND MEDIATOR PREPARATION

Pete Palmer is widely regarded as one of the top mediators in Indiana. In a CLE presentation titled *Planning Your First Personal Injury Case: First Personal Injury Mediation – Pete Palmer's Top Nine Tips for Successful Mediation*, Palmer discussed how to prepare your case for a successful mediation. From that list, I have highlighted what I believe are the two most important.

First, ensure you have the final amounts owed on all of the client's medical bills. Before every mediation at Isaacs & Isaacs, the chief Indiana litigator would have me call each medical provider our client visited to confirm the final balances owed prior to the mediation.

The second tip is to prepare the mediator. I recall mediator Larry Church once thanking me for consistently providing a detailed mediation statement. That statement included a breakdown of the total charges from each medical provider, along with the outstanding balance for each bill. I also attached to the mediation statement any relevant documentation I believed would help resolve the case. When sending my mediation statement, I typically included a note in the email authorizing the mediator to share any portion of the statement with defense counsel if he believed doing so would assist in reaching a resolution.

Mediation statements, typically submitted to the mediator by both counsels before the session, outline each party's position, summarize case facts, detail medical bills, and highlight key settlement issues. In my mediation statements, I include both the total billed amount and the outstanding balance for each medical provider, as well as the total lien amounts and current amounts owed after reductions. This detailed approach ensures the mediator has a clear, accurate understanding of the client's medical bills and liens, facilitating a fair and informed settlement.

WHY TRIAL PREPARATION DRIVES SETTLEMENT

A critical point emphasized in *The Complete Personal Injury Practice Manual* is that, particularly in cases involving substantial injuries, a meaningful settlement offer often doesn't materialize until the trial date is approaching. As the authors explain: "We do not expect to have much success in settling your lawsuit, especially if you have significant injuries, until we are close to the trial date. Only at that point does the insurance carrier typically have complete information to evaluate the case. Without that information, the carrier is not in a position to properly assess the case."

This principle is widely echoed by top personal injury attorneys, many of whom advise treating every case as if it will go to trial the moment a lawsuit is filed. Doing so demonstrates to the insurance carrier that you are fully committed to litigation, which can increase the likelihood of receiving a fair and timely settlement offer.

For example, Attorney Evan Aidman, in his book *Winning Personal Injury Cases*, stated, "Experienced lawyers are aware that in cases involving serious injuries, full value will probably not be offered until the discovery process has run its course." Likewise, Steven Burris, in *Automobile Accident Cases in Las Vegas*, notes, "Very oftentimes on the bigger cases, especially, the insurance company will not make a fair offer until a couple weeks before trial is to begin."

REACHING SETTLEMENT: A POLICY LIMITS VICTORY

Now let's turn to our mock case. I have great news: we did it – we secured a policy limits offer. After a long and hard-fought battle, the insurance company has finally agreed to settle for the policy limits in our mock Lisa Sampson case, offering the $25,000 policy limits.

Here's a quick refresher on how we achieved this result. On June 1, 2024, Lisa was injured in a car accident caused by Snake Jailbreak, who, after a night of drinking, drove recklessly and crashed into her, inflicting multiple painful injuries that disrupted her college career. After obtaining Lisa's medical bills and records, our firm prepared and sent an incredibly thorough demand packet in October 2024. This packet detailed Lisa's injuries through her medical documentation, included proof of her lost wages, linked the defendant's criminal probable cause affidavit to our civil claim, provided video and images of the accident scene, and featured a compelling demand letter that emphasized the human impact of the crash and how profoundly it affected Lisa's life.

In response to our demand packet, Unique Insurance made an initial offer of $14,300. After careful consideration, we rejected that offer and filed a lawsuit in January 2025. Once the lawsuit was filed, Unique Insurance asked our firm to hold off on pursuing further litigation until they could provide a new offer – a request we agreed to. In May 2025, Unique Insurance increased its offer to $22,000; however, given the serious nature of the case and the clear liability, we remained committed to obtaining the full policy limits and proceeded with discovery.

To increase pressure on the defense, we served interrogatories and scheduled the defendant's deposition. When these discovery efforts did not produce a policy limits offer, we filed a motion in August 2025 requesting a pretrial conference to set a trial date, further increasing the defense's exposure to additional litigation and costs. Soon after we requested a trial date, Unique Insurance made the logical decision to offer the full $25,000 policy limits.

Nearly every case I've handled has involved a fierce struggle to get the insurance company to pay a fair settlement. My hope is that the strategies and techniques I've shared throughout this book will give you an edge in your own practice – equipping you to fight more effectively than many plaintiff's attorneys who haven't had access to this level of insight. This $25,000 policy limits offer illustrates that even when your client's injuries are not catastrophic and their medical bills are relatively modest, you can still secure a full policy limits settlement. By presenting a clear, well-supported case for why the limits are warranted and applying strategic pressure on the defense, you can maximize the value of the claim and reach a just outcome for your client.

KEY SETTLEMENT DOCUMENTS

At the conclusion of a personal injury case, several key settlement documents are typically exchanged. These may include a cover letter from defense counsel requesting that the plaintiff sign a release, the release itself, a W-9 form, and a motion and order to dismiss the case. Defense counsel frequently requests a completed W-9 so the insurer can comply with IRS reporting requirements.

In some cases, especially those involving multiple defendants, you may also encounter a stipulation of partial dismissal. This document is used when you reach a settlement with one defendant but continue litigating against others. It allows the settled party to be dismissed from the case while preserving your claims against the remaining defendants.

DISBURSING SETTLEMENT FUNDS

To deposit a settlement check into your firm's trust account, you must first have the client sign a limited power of attorney authorizing you to do so. This document grants you the authority to endorse and deposit the check on the client's behalf. Once the full settlement amount has been deposited into your trust account, you can then issue disbursement checks to the appropriate parties—including the client, any lienholders, and your firm for attorney fees and case expenses.

It is also best practice to prepare a settlement disbursement instructions form. This form outlines the total settlement amount, the deductions for attorney fees and costs, payments to lienholders or medical providers, and the final dollar amount the client will receive. After reviewing the form with the client, you should have them sign it to confirm their understanding and approval of the disbursement. This step helps ensure transparency and protects your firm from any future disputes regarding how the funds were allocated.

THE SETTLEMENT CHECK

When defense counsel asks how the settlement check should be issued, instruct them to make it payable to both your client and your law firm. For example, in our mock case the insurer would issue the check to "Lisa Sampson and Leatherbury Law Office, LLC." Upon receipt, the settlement funds must be deposited into your firm's IOLTA (Interest on Lawyers' Trust Account) account.

TAX TREATMENT OF SETTLEMENT PROCEEDS

As a personal injury attorney, it is essential to understand the tax implications of settlements, as the tax treatment varies depending on the nature of the damages awarded. The Indiana-based personal injury firm Keller & Keller offers a helpful explanation of these issues on their website.

Generally, compensation for property damage is not subject to taxation. Similarly, settlement amounts allocated to medical expenses are typically treated as reimbursements and are therefore not taxable. Compensation for physical pain and suffering is also generally excluded from taxable income.

However, any portion of the settlement attributed to lost wages is considered taxable income. In summary, while most compensation for physical injuries and property damage is tax-exempt, amounts allocated to lost wages are subject to federal and state income taxes. This is because lost wage payments are treated the same as if the plaintiff had earned the income at work, whereas compensation for medical expenses and pain and suffering is viewed as making the plaintiff whole for personal injuries, which is excluded from gross income under Internal Revenue Code § 104(a)(2).

SUMMARY OF LISA SAMPSON'S CASE FOR MODULE 9

In Lisa Sampson's personal injury case, mediation was ultimately not required. Although mediation can be a valuable tool in many cases, our legal team determined that it would not be productive in this instance. Given the strength of the liability element, the egregious conduct of Snake, our young client's disrupted college career, and Lisa's medical bill totals, we believed the case warranted the full $25,000 policy limits and were not willing to compromise for anything less. As a result, mediation would have only added unnecessary time and expense and could have signaled to the defense that we were open to settling for less than full value – which we were not.

Instead, our legal team continued direct negotiations with defense counsel. After receiving responses to interrogatories and requests for production, and following our request for a trial date, defense counsel extended a policy-limits settlement offer of $25,000. This offer represented the maximum coverage available under the defendant's auto policy and underscored the strength of Lisa's claim.

Once the settlement was finalized, Lisa signed a release of all claims, which was provided to defense counsel. We also had Lisa sign a limited power of attorney authorizing our firm to deposit the settlement check, which was made payable to both Lisa and our firm. A detailed disbursement sheet was prepared outlining attorney fees, case costs, lien payments, and Lisa's net recovery. Lisa reviewed and signed the disbursement instructions, confirming her approval. Additionally, a motion and order to dismiss the case were filed with the court, officially closing the matter.

Pursuant to the 40% contingency fee agreement, $10,000 of the settlement proceeds was allocated to attorney's fees. Chambers Medical Group received $2,500 to satisfy its lien, and $828.90 was reimbursed to our firm for expenses. After these deductions, Lisa's take-home amount was $11,671.10.

Lisa's $11,671.10 disbursement was achieved by effectively negotiating multiple medical liens—including securing full lien waivers from her health insurer and MedPay carrier, as well as securing write-offs from her medical providers.

To view the Settlement Disbursement Instructions, please refer to Exhibit 10.

END OF MODULE 9

This concludes Module 9. In Module 10, I will walk you through some of the common pleadings typically filed in the lead-up to trial.

PRE-TRIAL MOTIONS

INTRODUCTION TO MODULE 10

In Module 10, we will address pretrial motions. A pretrial motion is a formal request by a party for the court to resolve an issue before trial. I have intentionally excluded trial proceedings from this book, as they warrant a separate, dedicated training course. Nevertheless, I will list examples of documentation you will likely need to file in a personal injury case as it nears the trial date, allowing you to become knowledgeable of these filings.

FINAL WITNESS AND EXHIBIT LISTS

As trial approaches, courts typically require each party to submit final witness and exhibit lists, often as part of the case management order. These lists must identify the individuals each side intends to call as witnesses and the documents, photographs, or other materials that are planned to be to introduced into evidence.

Once these lists are filed with the court, each party has the opportunity to review the opposing side's proposed exhibits and witnesses. They may then file objections through their Motions in Limine, specifying the legal grounds for each.

This pretrial process helps clarify what evidence and testimony will be permitted at trial and allows the court to rule on contested issues in advance, promoting a more efficient and orderly proceeding.

MOTIONS IN LIMINE

A motion in limine is a pretrial motion that asks the court to exclude or limit certain evidence from being presented to the jury. These motions are typically filed by both parties before trial begins to resolve evidentiary disputes in advance, ensuring that inadmissible or potentially prejudicial material is never shown to the jury. Unlike objections made during trial, which occur in real time and in front of the jury, motions in limine allow counsel to address these issues outside the jury's presence.

The motion must specifically identify the evidence to be excluded—such as witness statements, documents, photographs, or expert opinions—and provide a legal basis for its exclusion. Supporting the motion with statutes, case law, or rules of evidence is essential. For example, in an auto accident case, a plaintiff's attorney may file a motion in limine to bar the defense from introducing evidence of the plaintiff's prior driving record. The argument would be that such evidence could unfairly prejudice the jury.

In practice, motions in limine often seek to prevent the jury from hearing matters that are irrelevant or prejudicial to the claim—such as unrelated prior injuries, arguments that a large verdict would increase insurance rates, references to settlement negotiations, evidence of the defendant's insurance coverage, testimony or exhibits not disclosed in discovery, assertions of fraud, references to other lawsuits involving the plaintiff, or mention of the defendant's financial status. The purpose of such a request is to keep the trial focused on admissible evidence directly related to the issues at hand, while avoiding distractions or unfair inferences that could mislead the jury.

Another common target of motions in limine are so-called "Golden Rule" arguments and "Reptile Theory" tactics. A Golden Rule argument occurs when counsel asks jurors to place themselves in the plaintiff's position and award damages based on what they would want if they had suffered the same injuries. Courts almost universally prohibit this approach because it appeals to the jurors' personal interests rather than their duty to impartially evaluate the evidence. Similarly, Reptile Theory is a trial strategy in which plaintiff's counsel emphasizes community safety and jurors' role in protecting themselves and others by punishing the defendant. Defense attorneys frequently move in limine to exclude these arguments on the grounds that they improperly inflame the jury and shift the focus away from the facts and law of the case.

Mastering motions in limine is a key part of trial preparation, as these rulings can significantly shape the scope of the trial and what the jury is ultimately allowed to see and hear. A well-drafted motion in limine ensures that improper evidence is excluded before it ever reaches the jury, reducing the risk of reversible error and promoting a fair trial.

JURY INSTRUCTIONS

Jury instructions are a written set of directives that the judge reads to the jury at the beginning and end of trial. They are essential to the trial process, as they guide the jury in understanding their role and explain the legal standards they must apply when evaluating the facts and reaching a verdict.

In personal injury cases, jury instructions typically address key legal concepts such as negligence, burden of proof, causation, and damages. These instructions are often drawn from a set of standardized pattern jury instructions. Pattern instructions are developed by committees composed of judges, attorneys, and legal scholars who review current case law and translate complex legal principles into clear, straightforward language that jurors can understand.

Below are four sample jury instructions from a case I tried in Floyd County, Indiana, to give you a sense of how they are structured. In that case, the judge ultimately gave the jury a total of 23 instructions.

FINAL INSTRUCTION NO. 8

A party may present testimony by way of written or videotaped deposition.

A deposition is the sworn testimony of a witness taken before trial. The witness is placed under oath and swears to tell the truth, and the lawyer for each party may ask questions. A court reporter is present and records all the questions and answers.

Evaluate this testimony using the same rules you apply to testimony of other witnesses.

FINAL INSTRUCTION NO. 11

If you decide from the greater weight of the evidence that Defendant is liable to Plaintiff, then you must decide the amount of money that will fairly compensate Plaintiff. In deciding the amount of money you award, you may consider:

1. the nature and extent of the injuries, and the effect of the injuries on the Plaintiff's ability to function as a whole person; and

2. whether the injuries are temporary or permanent.

3. the physical pain and mental suffering Plaintiff has experienced and will experience in the future as a result of the injury

4. the reasonable value of necessary medical care, treatment, and services plaintiff incurred, and will incur in the future, as a result of the injuries;

5. the aggravation of a previous condition; and

6. The life expectancy of Plaintiff.

FINAL INSTRUCTION NO. 14

In deciding this case, you must not consider or speculate about whether either party has insurance.

FINAL INSTRUCTION NO. 16

Defendant is not excused from responsibility just because Plaintiff had a physical or mental condition at the time of the collision that made her more likely to be injured.

CONCLUSION

As you reach the conclusion of this book and reflect on the journey through our mock personal injury case, I want to thank you for your engagement with the material. This book was designed to provide you with actionable strategies drawn from the expertise of some of the nation's most accomplished personal injury attorneys. With these insights, you are well-prepared to confidently apply best practices at every stage of an auto accident case—from the initial car wreck to the settlement check.

LIST OF EXHIBITS

- ► **EXHIBIT 1**   Intake Form
- ► **EXHIBIT 2**   Indiana Officer's Standard Crash Report
- ► **EXHIBIT 3**   Path of Plaintiff Lisa Sampson's Vehicle
- ► **EXHIBIT 4**   Path of Defendant Snake Jailbreak's Vehicle
- ► **EXHIBIT 5**   The Demand Letter
- ► **EXHIBIT 6**   Picture of Plaintiff Lisa Sampson's Vehicle
- ► **EXHIBIT 7**   Complaint
- ► **EXHIBIT 8**   Appearance
- ► **EXHIBIT 9**   Summons
- ► **EXHIBIT 10**   Settlement Disbursement Instructions

EXHIBIT 1

INTAKE FORM

Name: Lisa Sampson
Address: 207 Ellen Ct., New Albany, IN 47150
Phone: 812-844-2496
Email: LisaSampson@gmail.com
Age: 20
DOB: 5/20/2004
SSN: 000-00-0000
Marital Status: Single
Spouse:
Children: None

Employer: Home Depot
Missed work as a result of the accident: Yes
Location: New Albany, IN
Group ID/Policy No.:

Health Insurance: Anthem
Group ID/Policy No.:

Your Auto Insurance Company: Erie Insurance
Adjuster:
Claim/Policy #:
Phone:

At-Fault Driver's Insurance: Unique Insurance
Adjuster:
Claim/Policy #:
Phone:

Facts of the Accident

Date: June 1, 2024
Time: 11pm
Weather: Clear
Location of Accident: Jeffersonville
Description: I was driving and got hit by a drunk driver

Medical Information

Injuries: I have pain in my hip, back, and neck and bruising
Ambulance Service: Yellow Ambulance
ER Facility: Clark Memorial
Medical Providers: Strickland, Cox, and Associates; Chambers Medical
Prior Injuries/Conditions: None

Additional Materials To Bring To Your Consultation

Please bring any of the following information and/or documentation which you have available. You are not required to bring any of these materials to your consultation. The additional materials you bring will help us to determine the status of your case, but at this time it is not necessary for you to request materials you do not have available.

- Police Report
- Photographs
- Names and contact information of parties involved
- Health Insurance Cards
- Work Excuses/Correspondence from your doctors
- Time missed from work, documentation of earnings, and date of hire
- Medical Records
- Medical Bills
- Documentation of any out-of-pocket expenses
- Property Damage Estimates

EXHIBIT 2

INDIANA OFFICER'S STANDARD CRASH REPORT
Electronic Version

	Page	1	of	4

Local ID

Date of Crash	Day of Week	Actual Local Time	County	Township	# Motor Vehicles	# Injured	# Dead	# Commercial Vehicles	# Deer
06/01/2024	SAT	11:10 PM	Clark	Jeffersonville	2	2	0	0	0

Road Crash Occurred On	Nearest/Intersecting Road/MilelMarker/Interchange	If not an intersection, number of feet from	Direction	Road Classification
Penn St	8TH St			LOCAL/CITY ROAD

Inside Corporate Limits?	City/Town or Nearest City/Town	Property?	Crash Latitude	Crash Longitude
YES	Jeffersonville			

Driver #1	Driver #2	Driver #3	Driver #4
Snake Jailbreak	Lisa Sampson		

Driver Contributing Circumstances

	Primary Cause	Vehicle 1	Vehicle 2	Vehicle 3	Vehicle 4
Alcoholic Beverages					
Illegal Drugs					
Prescription Drugs					
Driver Asleep or Fatigued					
Driver Illness					
Unsafe Speed					
Failure to Yield	✓	✓			
Disregard Signal					
Left of Center					
Improper Passing					
Improper Turning					
Improper Lane Usage					
Following Too Closely					
Unsafe Backing					
Overcorrecting					
Ran off Road					
Wrong Way on One Way					
Pedestrian's Action					
Passenger Distraction					
Restriction Violation					
Jackknifing					
Cell Phone Usage					
Other Telematics					
Driver Distracted					
Speed/Weather Conditions					
Unsafe Lane Movement					
Other					
None		✓			

Vehicle Contributing Circumstances

	Primary Cause	Vehicle 1	Vehicle 2	Vehicle 3	Vehicle 4
Engine Failure or Defective					
Accelerator Failure or Defective					
Brake Failure or Defective					
Tire Failure or Defective					
Headlight(s) Defective or Not On					
Other Lights Defective					
Steering Failure					
Window/Windshield Defective					
Oversize/Overweight Load					
Insecure/Leaky Load					
Tow Hitch Failure					
Other					
None			✓		

Environment Contributing Circumstances

	Primary Cause	Vehicle 1	Vehicle 2	Vehicle 3	Vehicle 4
Glare					
Roadway Surface					
Holes/Ruts in Surface					
Shoulder Defective					
Road Under Construction					
Severe Crosswinds					
Obstruction Not Marked					
Lane Marking Obscured					
View Obstructed					
Animal/Object in Roadway					
Traffic Ctl Inop/Missing/Obscure					
Utility Work					
Other					
None	✓	✓			

Area Information

Hit and Run	YES
School Zone	NO
Rumble Strips	NO
Locality	URBAN
Light Condition	DARK (LIGHTED)
Weather Conditions	CLEAR
Surface Condition	DRY
Type of Median	
Type of Roadway Junction	NO JUNCTION INVOLVED
Road Character	STRAIGHT/LEVEL
Roadway Surface	ASPHALT
Construction	NO
If Yes, Construction Type	
Traffic Control Devices	TRAFFIC CONTROL SIGNAL
Traffic Control Device Operational?	YES

Total Estimate of all damage in the Crash:
$10,001 to $25000

Was this crash the result of aggressive driving? NO

Other Property Damage (1)	State Property	Owner's Name and Address
Other Property Damage (2)	State Property	Owner's Name and Address

Witness/Other Participant

	#	Name
✓ Witness / Other Participant	1	Liv Bouvier

Address etc.

Phone #	Location at Time of Crash
812883000	INTERSECTION OF CRASH

	#	Name
Witness / Other Participant		Pedro Chespirito

Address etc.

Phone #	Location at Time of Crash
8128448056	

Non-Motorist

(Last Name, First Name, MI)	

Non Motorist Type	Non Motorist Action

Apparent Physical Condition	

Cited?	Direction	

Street/Highway

Traffic Control?	If yes, was traffic control operational?

Local ID

Type of Crash

Time Notified	Time Arrived	Other Location of Investigation				
11:15 PM	11:25 PM	AT SCENE ONLY				
Assisting Officer			ID No.	Agency	Investigation Complete?	Photos Taken?
				JEFFERSONVILLE PD	YES	YES
Assisting Officer			ID No.	Agency	Date of Report	
Investigating Officer			ID No.	Agency	Reviewing Officer	
Chief Wiggum						

Narrative

Driver of V1 was heading East on E. 8th St when he ran the red light striking V2 which was heading South on Penn St. D1 fled the scene on foot.

Driver of V2 was heading South on Penn St with the green light when she was struck by V1 who was heading East on E 8th St.

Passenger of V1 stated D1 was the driver of the vehicle and he had been drinking by her own admission.

Both Passenger1 and D2 were transported to the hospital for medical clearance. Jeffersonville

EXHIBIT 2   139

UNIT INFORMATION

Local ID

Page 3 of 4

	Driver's Name (Last, First, MI)	Safety Equipment Used
1	Jailbreak, Snake	

Address (Street, City, State, Zip)	Safety Equipment Effective?
93 Palm Avenue,	N/A
New Albany, IN 47150 IN 47150	Ejection/Trapped

Date of Birth	Age	Gender	EMS No.	Inmed Attn	Driver Injury Status
		MALE			

Driver's License #	Lic Type	CDL Class	Lic State	Nature of Most Severe Injury
1260-18-9999			IN	

Apparent Physical Status

- [ ] Normal
- [ ] Had Been Drinking
- [ ] Handicapped
- [ ] Ill
- [ ] Asleep/Fatigued
- [ ] Drugs/Medication
- [x] Unknown

Restrictions

- [ ] Glasses/Contact Lenses
- [ ] Outside Rearview Mirror
- [ ] Daylight Driving
- [ ] Automatic Transmission
- [ ] Special Controls
- [ ] Employment Only
- [ ] Motorcycle Only
- [ ] To/From Employment
- [ ] Employer's Vehicle Only
- [ ] State-Owned Vehicles
- [ ] PP Chauffeurs Taxi Only
- [ ] Power Steering
- [ ] Special Restrictions
- [ ] Probation DWI
- [ ] Probation HTO
- [x] None

Location of Most Severe Injury

If Cited?
- [ ] Infraction
- [x] Misdemeanor
- [ ] Felony

IC Codes
9-18-1-1

Test Given	Type Given
NONE	[ ] Blood [ ] Urine [ ] Breath [ ] SFST [ ] PBT

Alcohol Results	Certified Test		Drug Results
PBI	[ ] Pending		

Veh#	Color	Vehicle Year	Make	Model	Style
1	Blue	2004	Ford	F150	VN

# Occupants	Lic Year	License #	License State
2	2018		IN

# Axles	Speed Limit	Insured By	Phone Number
2	35	Unique Insurance Company	

Vehicle Identification #

Initial Impact Area
- [ ] Undercarriage
- [ ] Trailer
- [ ] None
- [x] Unknown

(Front / Rear diagram)

Registered Owner's Name (Last, First, MI)		[ ] Same as Driver
Bouvier, Liv		

Address (Street, City, State, Zip)

IN   47130

Areas Damaged (Multiples)
- [ ] Undercarriage: [x] [ ] [ ]
- [ ] Trailer: [x] [ ] [ ]
- [ ] None: [x] [x] [x]
- [ ] Unknown

(Front / Rear diagram)

Vehicle Use
PERSONAL (FARM, COMPANY)

Towed?	Company: Midnight Towboy	Due to Disabling Damage
YES		YES

Emergency Run?   Fire?
                                    NO

	Lic State	Lic Year	Registered Owner's Name (Last, First, MI)	[ ] Same as Driver
License#			Address (Street, City, State, Zip)	
Veh Year	Make			

Vehicle Type
PASSENGER CAR/STATION WAGON

Pre Crash Vehicle Action
GOING STRAIGHT

Direction of Travel
EAST

	Lic State	Lic Year	Registered Owner's Name (Last, First, MI)	[ ] Same as Driver
License#			Address (Street, City, State, Zip)	
Veh Year	Make			

Type of Primary/Secondary Roadway

- [ ] One Way Road
- [ ] One Lane - One Way
- [ ] Two Lanes - One Way
- [ ] Multi Lanes (3 or more) - One Way
- [ ] Multi-Lane w/ Grass Median Only
- [ ] Multi-Lane w/ Center Turn Lane
- [ ] Multi-Lane w/ Curb Raised Median
- [ ] Multi-Lane w/ Cable Barrier

- [x] Two Lanes - Two Way
- [ ] Multi Lane Divided (2 or more) - Two Way
- [ ] Multi-Lane Undivided Two Way Left Turn
- [ ] Multi-Lane Undivided (3 or more) - Two Way
- [ ] Multi-Lane w/ Concrete Barrier
- [ ] Multi-Lane w/ Metal Guardrail Median
- [ ] Private Drive   [ ] Alley
- [ ] Ramp

Commercial Vehicle: Carrier's Name and Address

HAZMAT Proper Shipping Name:	State DOT#
US DOT#	ICC#	CMV Inspection	If Yes

Event Collision With
1. ANOTHER MOTOR VEHICLE 2. UTILITY POLE

Gross Vehicle Weight Rating	Cargo Body Type

HAZMAT Placard	HAZMAT Release of Cargo	HAZMAT 4-Digit ID#	Hazzard Class #

3. OTHER - EXPLAIN IN NARRATIVE

UNIT INFORMATION

Local ID

	Driver's Name (Last, First, MI)	Safety Equipment Used
2	Sampson, Lisa	LAP + HARNESS

Address (Street, City, State, Zip)
207 Ellen Ct.

New Albany, IN 47150

Safety Equipment Effective?
YES

Ejection/Trapped
NOT EJECTED OR TRAPPED

Date of Birth	Age	Gender
05/10/2004	20	FEMALE

EMS No.	Inmed Attn	Driver Injury Status

Driver's License #	Lic Type	CDL Class	Lic State
	OP		IN

Nature of Most Severe Injury

Apparent Physical Status
- [x] Normal
- [ ] Had Been Drinking
- [ ] Handicapped
- [ ] Ill
- [ ] Asleep/Fatigued
- [ ] Drugs/Medication
- [ ] Unknown

Restrictions
- [ ] Glasses/Contact Lenses
- [ ] Outside Rearview Mirror
- [ ] Daylight Driving
- [ ] Automatic Transmission
- [ ] Special Controls
- [ ] Employment Only
- [ ] Motorcycle Only
- [ ] To/From Employment
- [ ] Employer's Vehicle Only
- [ ] State-Owned Vehicles
- [ ] PP Chauffeurs Taxi Only
- [ ] Power Steering
- [ ] Special Restrictions
- [ ] Probation DWI
- [ ] Probation HTO
- [x] None

Location of Most Severe Injury

If Cited?
- [ ] Infraction
- [ ] Misdemeanor
- [ ] Felony

IC Codes

Test Given	Type Given				
NONE	[ ] Blood	[ ] Urine	[ ] Breath	[ ] SFST	[ ] PBT

Alcohol Results			Drug Results
PBT	Certified Test	[ ] Pending	

Veh#	Color	Vehicle Year	Make	Model	Style
2	Red	2012	Ford	Mustang	4D

# Occupants	Lic Year	License #	License State
1			IN

# Axles	Speed Limit	Insured By	Phone Number
2	40	Erie Insurance	

Initial Impact Area
- [ ] Undercarriage
- [ ] Trailer
- [ ] None
- [x] (Front)
- [ ] Unknown

Vehicle Identification #

Registered Owner's Name (Last, First, MI)
Sampson, Lisa   [ ] Same as Driver

Address (Street, City, State, Zip)

IN   47201

Areas Damaged (Multiples)
- [ ] Undercarriage
- [x] Trailer (Front)
- [x] None (Front)
- [ ] Unknown

Vehicle Use
PERSONAL (FARM, COMPANY)

Towed?	Company: Midnight Towboy	Due to Disabling Damage
YES		YES

Lic State	Lic Year	Registered Owner's Name (Last, First, MI) [ ] Same as Driver

Emergency Run? | **Fire?** NO

License# | **Address (Street, City, State, Zip)**

Vehicle Type
PASSENGER CAR/STATION WAGON

Veh Year | Make

Pre Crash Vehicle Action
GOING STRAIGHT

Lic State	Lic Year	Registered Owner's Name (Last, First, MI) [ ] Same as Driver

Direction of Travel
EAST

License# | **Address (Street, City, State, Zip)**

Veh Year | Make

Type of Primary/Secondary Roadway
- [ ] One Way Road
- [ ] One Lane - One Way
- [ ] Two Lanes - One Way
- [ ] Multi Lanes (3 or more) - One Way
- [ ] Multi-Lane w/ Grass Median Only
- [x] Multi Lane w/ Center Turn Lane
- [ ] Multi Lane w/ Curb Raised Median
- [ ] Multi Lane w/ Cable Barrier
- [ ] Two Lanes - Two Way
- [ ] Multi-Lane Divided (2 or more) - Two Way
- [ ] Multi Lane Undivided Two Way Left Turn
- [ ] Multi-Lane Undivided (3 or more) - Two Way
- [ ] Multi Lane w/ Concrete Barrier
- [ ] Multi Lane w/ Metal Guardrail Median
- [ ] Private Drive   [ ] Alley
- [ ] Ramp

Commercial Vehicle: Carrier's Name and Address

HAZMAT Proper Shipping Name	State DOT#

US DOT#	ICC#	CMV Inspection	If Yes

Event Collision With
1. ANOTHER MOTOR VEHICLE

Gross Vehicle Weight Rating	Cargo Body Type

HAZMAT Placard	HAZMAT Release of Cargo	HAZMAT 4-Digit ID#	Hazzard Class #

EXHIBIT 2   141

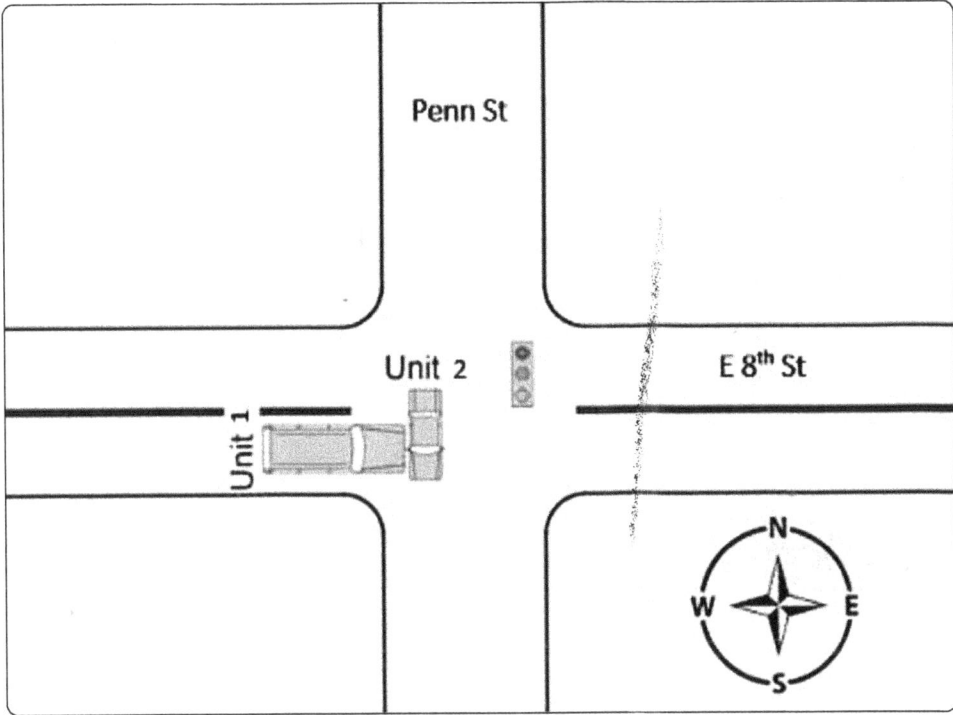

Penn St

Unit 2

Unit 1

E 8th St

N

W   E

S

EXHIBIT 3

POINT OF VIEW OF LISA: Lisa was traveling southbound on Penn Street with a green light as she approached the intersection.

EXHIBIT 4

POINT OF VIEW OF SNAKE: Snake was traveling eastbound on 8th Street and failed to stop at the red traffic signal before entering the intersection.

EXHIBIT 5

THE DEMAND LETTER

October 10, 2024

Ms. Edna Krabappel
Unique Insurance
7400 North Caldwell Avenue
Niles, Illinois 60714

      Re: Our Client: Lisa Sampson
               Date of Accident: June 1, 2024
               Your Insured: Patty Bouvier
               Claim No.: 000000001

Dear Ms. Krabappel:

Lisa Sampson sustained serious injuries on June 1, 2024, when your insured, Snake Jailbreak, ran a red light at the intersection of East 8th Street and Penn Street in Jeffersonville, Indiana. At the time, Lisa was lawfully traveling southbound on Penn Street with a green light when your insured violently collided with her vehicle. The police report concludes that your insured's failure to yield the right of way caused the collision. Furthermore, Snake Jailbreak was under the influence of alcohol at the time of the crash and fled the scene, resulting in criminal charges, copies of which are enclosed for your review. The impact was so severe that it totaled Lisa's 2012 Mustang and required her to be transported by ambulance to Clark Memorial Hospital. The ambulance report states that Lisa's vehicle was propelled 30 yards down the street.

EXHIBIT 5   145

At Clark Memorial Hospital, Lisa was treated for hip pain, bruising to her thigh, neck pain, back pain, and wrist pain. Notably, Lisa is only 5'3" and weighs 120 pounds. Lisa was discharged from the hospital with crutches and referred to her primary care physician, who ordered an extensive course of physical therapy at Chambers Medical Group immediately. At her initial evaluation, Lisa received multiple diagnoses related to injuries to her spine and hip. The Chambers Medical Group records clearly state, "Patient's past medical history is nonrelated," and that her "back pain began immediately after the accident." Between June 4, 2024, and October 4, 2024, Lisa completed twenty-seven therapy sessions to address her accident-related injuries.

Lisa's pain and limitations have been significant and are well documented in her medical records. She was unable to return to work immediately, and the collision severely disrupted her college career, forcing her to miss substantial coursework. Prior to the crash, Lisa was an exceptional student; she has since had to seek special permission from her professors to make up her assignments and exams.

To date, Lisa's medical bills total $13,000.00, all of which were incurred directly as a result of your insured's gross negligence. Based on the undisputed facts outlined above, please accept this letter as our formal demand for payment of the full policy limits, which we understand to be only $25,000.

Sincerely,
/s/ Clarence Leatherbury
Leatherbury Law Office
201 N Main Street, Salem, IN 47167
812-883-2292
LeatherburyLaw@gmail.com

EXHIBIT 6

LISA SAMPSON'S VEHICLE

EXHIBIT 7

IN THE _____COURT FOR CLARK COUNTY
STATE OF INDIANA

LISA SAMPSON	)	
Plaintiff,	)	
	)	
v.	)	CAUSE NO: _____
	)	*ELECTRONICALLY FILED*
SNAKE JAILBREAK	)	
93 Palm Avenue	)	
New Albany, Indiana 47150	)	
Defendant.	)	
	)	
	)	

COMPLAINT AND DEMAND FOR JURY TRIAL

Comes now the Plaintiff, Lisa Sampson, by counsel, Leatherbury Law Office, and for cause of action against the Defendant, Snake Jailbreak, alleges and says:

1. That on or about June 1, 2024, the Defendant, Snake Jailbreak, negligently drove his vehicle, causing his vehicle to strike the vehicle driving by the Plaintiff, Lisa Sampson.
2. That said collision occurred within the boundaries of Clark County, State of Indiana.
3. That the Plaintiff received permanent injuries, pain, suffering, and anguish as a result of the Defendant's negligence.

4. That the Plaintiff has incurred medical expenses, lost wages, property damage including, but not limited to, diminished value, and other special expenses in an amount to be proven at the trial of this cause, and will incur future medical expenses, lost wages and other special expenses, as a direct and proximate result of defendant's negligence.

WHEREFORE, the Plaintiff demands judgment against the Defendant for permanent injuries in a reasonable amount to be determined at the trial of this cause, for medical expenses, lost wages, property damage including, but not limited to, diminished value, and other special expenses, for future medical expenses, lost wages and other special expenses, court costs, and all other proper relief in the premises.

By: /s/ Clarence B. Leatherbury
        Clarence B. Leatherbury
        Attorney for Plaintiff Lisa Sampson

        Leatherbury Law Office
        201 N. Main St.
        Salem, IN 47167
        Telephone: (812)883-2292
        Facsimile: (812) 883-2210
        Email: LeatherburyLaw@gmail.com

DEMAND FOR JURY TRIAL

Comes now the Plaintiff, by counsel, Leatherbury Law Office, and request that this matter be tried by jury pursuant to Indiana Trial Rule 38.

        /s/ Clarence B. Leatherbury
        Clarence B. Leatherbury, #32660-88

IN THE _____ COURT FOR CLARK COUNTY
STATE OF INDIANA

LISA SAMPSON	)	
Plaintiff,	)	
	)	
v.	)	CAUSE NO: _____
	)	*ELECTRONICALLY FILED*
SNAKE JAILBREAK	)	
93 Palm Avenue	)	
New Albany, Indiana 47150	)	
Defendant.	)	
	)	
	)	

APPEARANCE BY ATTORNEY IN CIVIL CASE

1. Initiating Party: Lisa Sampson
2. Attorney Information: Clarence B. Leatherbury, #32660-88
   Leatherbury Law Office
   201 N. Main St., Salem, IN 47167
   Telephone: (812) 883-2292
   Email: LeatherburyLaw@gmail.com
3. Are there other party members?   No.
4. Case type requested: Civil Tort (CT)
5. Accept: (a) Fax Service: No.
              (b) Courthouse Mailbox: No.
6. Does this case involve support issues?   No.

7. Are there related cases?   No.

8. Additional Information: None.

/s/ Clarence B. Leatherbury
Leatherbury Law Office
201 N. Main St., Salem, IN 47167
Telephone: (812) 883-2292
Email: LeatherburyLaw@gmail.com
Counsel for Plaintiff Lisa Sampson

IN THE _____ COURT FOR CLARK COUNTY

STATE OF INDIANA

LISA SAMPSON	)	
Plaintiff,	)	
	)	
v.	)	CAUSE NO: _____
	)	*ELECTRONICALLY FILED*
SNAKE JAILBREAK	)	
93 Palm Avenue	)	
New Albany, Indiana 47150	)	
Defendant.	)	
	)	
	)	

SUMMONS

THE STATE OF INDIANA TO: Snake Jailbreak

ADDRESS: 93 Palm Avenue

New Albany, IN 47150

You are hereby notified that you have been sued by the person(s) or entity(ies) named as Plaintiff(s) in the court and case number indicated in the above caption.

The Plaintiff is represented in this action by: Clarence Leatherbury, Leatherbury Law Office, 201 N. Main St., Salem, IN 47167, telephone: (812) 883-2292.

The nature of the suit against you is stated in the complaint that is attached to this summons. It also states the relief sought or the demand made against you by the Plaintiff.

An answer or other appropriate response in writing to the complaint must be filed either by you or your attorney within twenty (20) days, commencing the day after you receive this summons *(or twenty-three (23) days if this summons was received by mail)*, or a judgment by default may be rendered against you for relief demanded by Plaintiff.

The following manner of service of Summons is hereby designated:

CERTIFIED MAIL

Dated: _____

_____
Clark County Clerk *(Seal)*

SETTLEMENT DISBURSEMENT INSTRUCTIONS

Client Name: Lisa Sampson
Date: March 1, 2025
File #: 2077
Assigned Attorney: Clarence Leatherbury

Disbursement Instructions

Insurance Check:

1.   Insurance Co. Name: Unique Insurance
     Amount: $25,000.00
     Attorney Fee Percentage: 40%

Pay the following lienholders and medical providers from Settlement:

1.   Lien Holder Name: Chambers Medical Group
     Amount: $2,500.00
     Make check payable to: Chambers Medical Group.
     Mail check to: 4072 Taylorsville Rd, Louisville, KY 40220

Settlement Breakdown

$25,000
-10,000 40% Contract Fee
-2,500 Chambers Medical Group Lien
 -828.90 DTF

_____

=11,671.10 to client

Settlement Notes:

- ► Erie Insurance (MedPay) reduced their lien to zero
- ► Anthem Health Insurance reduced their lien to zero
- ► Clark Memorial Hospital lien hasn't been recorded. Client stated she will pay on her own.
- ► All remaining medical provider balances are at $0
- ► On payment authorization form client checked direct deposit

Checklist

Release Signed?	Yes
Limited Power of Attorney signed?	Yes
Settlement Check received?	Yes

BOOKS MENTIONED

1. **Evan Aidman** - *Winning Personal Injury Cases*

2. **Michael Schafer** - *The Kentucky Accident Book: 7 Potholes That Can Wreck Your Kentucky Accident Case*

3. **Andrew Smiley** - *How to Successfully Litigate a Personal Injury Case*

4. **Al Cone & Verne Lawyer** - *The Complete Personal Injury Practice Manual*

5. **Guy DiMartino** - *A Guide to Indiana Car Accident Claims*

6. **Laura Ruhl Genson & Anita M. Kerezman (Editors)** - *Truck Accident Litigation*, Second Edition

7. **Paul Kruse & Tony Patterson** - *Indiana Accident Law: A Reference for Accident Victims*

8. **Steven Burris** - *Automobile Accident Cases In Las Vegas*

9. **Randall Sevenish** - *The Indiana Crash Book*

10. **Eric Kahn** - *Library of New Jersey Personal Injury Forms*, Third Edition

11. **Edward Swartz and Elly Swartz** - *Handbook of Personal Injury Forms and Litigation Materials*, Second Edition

12. **Joseph Fried and Michael Goldberg** - *Understanding Motor Carrier Claims*, Seventh Edition

www.ingramcontent.com/pod-product-compliance
Lightning Source LLC
Chambersburg PA
CBHW081816200326
41597CB00023B/4269